Business Skills for S

# Business Skills for Secretaries

## Jan Whitehead

Croner Publications Ltd
Croner House
London Road
Kingston upon Thames
Surrey KT2 6SR
Telephone: 081-547 3333

Copyright © 1992 J Whitehead
First published 1992
Reprinted 1992

Published by
Croner Publications Ltd,
Croner House,
London Road
Kingston upon Thames,
Surrey KT2 6SR
Telephone: 081-547 3333

While every care has been taken
in the writing and editing of this book,
readers should be aware that only Acts of Parliament
and Statutory Instruments have the force of law,
and that only the courts can authoritatively
interpret the law.

British Library Cataloguing in Publication Data
A CIP Catalogue Record for this book
is available from the British Library

ISBN 1-85524-084-X

Printed by Whitstable Litho Ltd, Whitstable, Kent

# Contents

# Preface

## Purpose of the book

In writing this book I have made assumptions about the kind of people who may find it useful. I envisage you as a hard working secretary or administrative assistant who has already undergone a secretarial course to acquire qualifications and who has a desire to do your existing job more effectively and/or wish to progress within your chosen career.

This book will not recap on the duties of a secretary which you have probably covered in subjects such as "secretarial duties" or "office practice"; however, it will cover a range of personal and interpersonal skills that will help you to:

(a) develop a satisfying working relationship with you manager
(b) communicate well with other managers, secretaries, visitors and clients
(c) organise your work efficiently
(d) plan your future career.

Several books have already been written for managers or management trainees on subjects such as time management, negotiation and handling awkward customers, yet it is often secretaries who help managers to be more effective in their relationships with others, both inside and outside the organisation. If you find this book helpful and can set a good example in your interpersonal skills, it will help your manager too — he or she may even want to borrow it from your bookshelf! I recommend this book as a reference text to be kept on your bookshelf alongside *Croner's Office Companion*. The latter can be used for easy access to useful reference information while this book can be used to "dip into" when you want to work on improving a particular personal or interpersonal skill.

## Organisation of the book

I have divided the book into six sections, each dealing with a specific skill area:

*Section 1* concentrates on some of the aspects which will enable you to have an effective working partnership with your manager.

*Sections 2 and 3* deal with the communication skills vital to successful relationships with all those inside and outside your organisation. Such communication may involve face to face encounters, telephone contact or written memos, letters, reports, press releases, etc. It enables you to deal with difficult encounters in a calm, assertive manner.

Since information processing is central to any manager/secretary relationship, *Section 4* helps you to research and use information more effectively and to adopt a logical approach to decision making.

Self-organisation and good time management are crucial to anyone who has to plan, organise and control workflow and therefore *Section 5* provides some useful hints on how to organise your time and avoid stress.

Finally, *Section 6* looks at your own future with some ideas on how you can plan your own career development.

## Layout of sections

At the beginning of each section, I have given a set of objectives I consider you will be able to achieve if you accept the information and practise the skills mentioned within that section.

I have tried to adopt a user-friendly style of writing and presenting information that allows you to extract ideas quickly and easily by keeping dense explanatory text to a minimum and making maximum use of tables, diagrams, checklists and action points.

At the end of each section you will find a "do and do not" list which summarises the main points in the section.

I trust that this book becomes dog-eared with constant use and that it helps you towards a positive and satisfying career.

Jan Whitehead<br>
October 1991

# Section 1

## The Working Relationship with your Manager

### Objectives

By the end of this section you will be able to:

(a) understand what is involved in a manager's role

(b) understand the role of the secretary or administrative assistant

(c) decide how you can best assist *your* manager to perform his or her role

(d) discuss your respective roles in a constructive and positive way so that you can achieve a harmonious working relationship

(e) clarify your expectations of one another so that you avoid misunderstandings.

# Chapter 1

## The Secretary's Role

### Traditional concepts

Secretaries and administrative assistants have traditionally been viewed as having certain practical skills, particularly in keyboarding. They were employed to relieve managers of the tedious aspects of dealing with correspondence, had a status that was considered inferior to that of their manager and had few opportunities for a career progression from a secretarial role to that of a manager. Perhaps this was typified by the comments made about them.

— "That's Mr Black's secretary."
— "My wife looks after my home; my secretary looks after my office."

The secretary was seen as a *possession* or an *appendage* of the manager.

— "Julie works for me."

The secretary was seen in a *subordinate, servile role.*

— "Secretaries are expensive ornaments that decorate the office and make polite conversation to visitors."

The secretary was seen as a *decorative addition.*

Also, the assumption used to be that this was an occupation exclusively suited to women.

Attitudes are now beginning to change:

(a) male secretaries and administrative assistants may still not be the norm but some men are finding this a rewarding career

(b) managers are discovering for themselves that the professional training given to many secretaries enables them to carry out a wide range of supportive activities which involve problem solving, decision making and planning

(c) secretaries are helping to change their own image by taking the initiative within their jobs to demonstrate to their managers the type of work of which they are capable

(d) more and more secretaries are making the progression from secretarial into managerial and professional roles.

If a secretary is to develop a fulfilling modern supportive role, the first step is to have a good understanding of the manager's function.

# Understanding the manager's role

Managers are likely to have been appointed to their positions partly for their technical expertise — this may be in employing people, selling, accounting, research, buying, etc. Some of a manager's time will obviously be spent carrying out tasks related to this specialisation.

However, there are some functions that all managers, regardless of their specialisation, share.

## *Managerial functions*

In a thesaurus, amongst other definitions, to manage is to "command", "superintend", or "be in charge of". A manager is therefore a person who is in charge of other people, equipment, money, etc.

There are some recognised functions that all managers will perform. It does not matter whether they work in an organisation in the public or private sector, in a large or small organisation, or whether the organisation is concerned with producing a product or providing a service; all managers should perform the functions shown in the table below.

**Management functions**

| Function | Description |
| --- | --- |
| Planning | Looking ahead and making decisions about what objectives the section or department should be achieving and how these objectives will be achieved. This will involve short term and long term plans. |
| Organising | Arranging the resources which are needed to fulfil plans, ie providing suitable people, materials, equipment, information. |
| Directing | Communicating with subordinates about carrying out their tasks, including giving instructions, advice, motivation. |
| Co-ordinating | Ensuring that all subordinates are working *together* effectively to achieve objectives and that the work of the section or department is linked to that of other sections and departments. |
| Controlling | Monitoring the performance of tasks by subordinates to ensure that plans are carried out and making adjustments as necessary. |

Although all managers' jobs will involve these functions, individual managers place different emphasis on particular functions. In order to

---

**Action**

A useful starting point in understanding the job of manager is to see where your own manager places his or her emphasis amongst these functions.

---

carry out these functions managers have to relate to their own superiors, other managers, clients, visitors and subordinates. Various studies have been carried out on how managers spend their time. The following pie chart shows the proportion of time spent on various activities in a typical manager's day.

*Figure 1 Pie chart showing how a manager may spend the day*

A large proportion of a manager's time is spent in informal or formal meetings — progress meetings, planning meetings, consultation with other managers, negotiating with people inside and outside the organisation, briefings, sessions with individuals or groups of subordinates, interviews for new staff. This leaves only a small proportion of time for desk work.

# Requirements of a good manager

To do their jobs well, managers require a range of knowledge, skills and qualities. You, no doubt, have your own ideas about what makes a good manager.

The table below shows the necessary qualities and skills which a number of secretaries suggested.

### Requirements of a good manager

| Knowledge of | Skills in | Qualities |
|---|---|---|
| own specialisation | decision making | positive attitude |
| the organisation — policies, procedures products and services | problem solving communicating | patient fair |
| the industry in which the organisation operates | team building leadership | in control of emotions |
| the social, political, economic and technological environment of the organisation | persuading delegating negotiating | |

Some individual comments were:

"I like a manager who is very clear about what he wants to achieve and how to attain it."

"I think someone who can communicate well makes a good manager; also, someone who is willing to ask for advice sometimes and believes in teamwork."

"I can respond well to a manager who is positive and enthusiastic about his or her job, doesn't get moody and is willing to give praise when it is earned."

It is a good idea to rate your manager's strengths and weaknesses.

---

**Action**

Go back to the list of requirements for a good manager on page 7.

Against each characteristic rate your own manager on a scale of 0-5 (0 for poor up to 5 for excellent).

---

This activity is not intended to encourage destructive criticism of managers or to provide ammunition for moaning about bad points.

If you are realistic about your manager's shortcomings, you can sometimes help him or her towards acquiring knowledge and developing a skill; furthermore, you may be able to compensate by showing the relevant skill or quality yourself. Complementing one another, in terms of knowledge, skills and qualities, is part of being an effective working partnership.

You are not likely to be the only person who needs to work harmoniously with your manager. All managers have subordinates — those people whose work they must plan, organise, direct, co-ordinate and control.

The tasks that these subordinates will carry out are a small part of the manager's own job responsibilities. Therefore all managers are involved in delegation.

## *Delegation*

When managers delegate they are:

   (a) identifying tasks for which they are responsible in their own jobs and passing down to subordinates the authority to make decisions relating to those tasks
   (b) holding the subordinates accountable to them for carrying out the tasks effectively
   (c) retaining ultimate responsibility for good performance themselves.

The following diagram illustrates the idea of delegation.

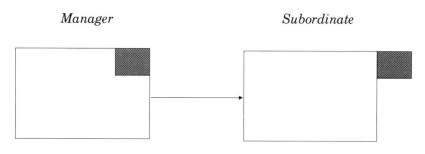

*Figure 2  Concept of delegation*

There are obvious advantages to both managers and subordinates if managers delegate tasks wisely.

## Advantages of delegation

| *To the manager it means:* | *To the subordinate it can mean:* |
|---|---|
| the work load is reduced | the opportunity to use abilities |
| there is more time to concentrate on the priority functions of management — to plan ahead | making the job more interesting and challenging |
| the opportunity to identify those subordinates who are suitable for promotion. | preparing them for jobs with greater authority. |

However, many managers cannot delegate very well. Some likely causes of poor delegation are:

(a) *fear*
    (i)    of giving too much scope to subordinates who might then challenge the manager's own position
    (ii)   that subordinates will make mistakes for which the manager will be responsible
(b) *withholding authority*
ie holding subordinates accountable for getting the task done but not delegating authority (the right to make decisions relating to the task) so that the subordinates cannot do the task properly and become frustrated
(c) *delegating inappropriate tasks*
ie delegating tasks which subordinates do not have the knowledge, skills or experience to carry out properly
(d) *poor control*
ie failing to monitor whether the subordinate is carrying out the task properly.

It may be difficult to help a manager with delegation affecting his or her other subordinates, although it should be possible occasionally to make a tactful suggestion along the lines of:

"You're so busy on planning the new product launch, can't ___ do that for you?"

Another delegation problem secretaries face is that managers may not recognise the knowledge, skills and experience they possess and therefore do not delegate tasks to them to any great extent. In this situation, it is necessary to discuss their job role seriously with their manager and possibly redefine the job description (see Chapter 2). In this respect secretaries must be very clear about the role they should be undertaking.

# The secretary's role

## *Formal position in authority structure*

The essential point about the secretary or administrative assistant's role is that he or she is there to assist managers to carry out their roles. The job of secretary is an extension of the manager's role. In this sense, a secretary has no formal organisational relationship with any of the manager's other subordinates. On an organisation chart, a true representation of the position would be as shown below.

**Organisation chart showing the secretary's formal role**

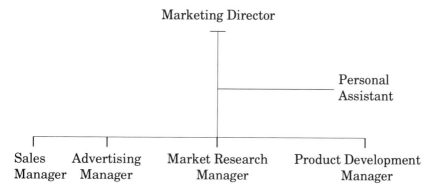

## *The secretary's areas of expertise*

A secretary's role is to help the manager carry out his or her job role. The main expertise in this relationship is knowledge of information processing — the secretary is an information centre, ie:

(a) *receiving information*
    (i)    controlling incoming post
    (ii)   receiving electronic mail
    (iii)  receiving incoming telephone calls/telex/fax
    (iv)  accessing external databases
(b) *recording information*
    (i)    typing
    (ii)   word processing
    (iii)  inputting information on computer
    (iv)  copying and printing
(c) *storing information*
    maintaining paper based or electronic filing systems

(d) *communicating information*
- (i)    sending memos, letters, reports, press releases
- (ii)   sending messages by post, fax, telex, telephone, electronic mail
- (iii)  conversations, meetings, interviews, oral reporting
- (iv)  using charts, diagrams, illustrations, symbols, signs.

In addition to these information processing functions which are the core of a secretary's expertise, he or she may, for example, have skills in:

- (a) handling people
- (b) entertaining
- (c) driving, or
- (d) foreign languages.

## Technology and the secretarial role

The development of computers and telecommunications equipment has provided people with great opportunities in the secretarial role — and, possibly, a major threat.

Old technology demanded that a large proportion of a secretary's time was spent taking and transcribing dictation, and typing correspondence, reports, etc. A secretary was hired for the ability to take shorthand or audio dictation and to type.

Modern equipment will allow the secretarial role to develop in two ways.

(a) *The secretary as an extension of the machine*
The equipment may be seen by managers as a machine which allows the secretary to deal with routine tasks more quickly and accurately. It is used to intensify all the routine aspects of the job.

(b) *The machine as a tool of the secretary*
Managers may use the full facilities of modern equipment so that the machines take over their routine tasks and those of their secretaries, leaving both free to concentrate on the more important pro-active functions of planning and organising.

If used as in (a), a good word processor operator, rather than a secretary, is all that is needed for the job. In the case of (b) the secretarial role can become one of the following:

(a) *researcher* — accessing data inside and outside the organisation
(b) *information processor* — taking the initiative in processing data into a format in which it can be used by the manager or stored so that the manager can make rational decisions at the appropriate time
(c) *planner and organiser* — taking over control of the day-to-day planning and organisation of information in the office which backs up managerial decision making and action (ie maintaining diaries, bring forward systems, planning aids, making appointments, organising meetings and conferences, arranging travel, receiving visitors, deflecting unwelcome callers).

The ambitious secretary should be aiming to fulfil this latter role. The two characteristics which distinguish a secretary from a "typist" or "word processor operator" are:

(a) the ability to use initiative
(b) the ability to think ahead — to anticipate.

Secretaries should not just be reacting to instructions but should be pro-active — planning ahead and organising their work and that of their managers to ensure that plans are fulfilled. Modern equipment should be the servant of the secretary, never the secretary the servant of the equipment.

## *The secretary's role relationships*

Although secretaries are there to support managers, this brings them into a complex pattern of relationships with a wide range of other people, both inside and outside the organisation. These people will make demands and it is necessary to maintain an effective relationship with them which reinforces the image of the manager and the employing organisation. Some of the skills that will enable a secretary to sustain satisfactory relationships are dealt with in the rest of this book.

Some of these role relationships are identified in the following table.

## The secretary's pattern of role relationships

| Role relationship | The manager's expectations of the secretary in these role relationships |
|---|---|
| Manager | Must show loyalty, be trustworthy and give total support. |
| Manager's subordinates | Must be pleasant, approachable, able to protect the manager from unnecessary interruptions and not gossip about him or her. |
| Other managers | Must be courteous and helpful but not be drawn into disclosing confidential information about the manager's work or life. |
| Other secretaries | Must share technical knowledge, support, professional status, be approachable and friendly but not gossip about the manager's work or life. |
| Junior clerical staff (subordinates) | Must be approachable, prepared to help with technical difficulties, delegate tasks which will help develop their abilities, control their work standards. |
| Junior clerical staff (others) | Must be polite and show appreciation of their efforts. |
| Manager's family | Must be courteous and helpful while not disclosing any privileged information about the manager's work. |
| Manager's close business associates | Must be courteous and helpful, provide relevant information when authorised but not be drawn into disclosing any unauthorised information. |
| Visitors | Must be polite and helpful to those with appointments and be prepared to be firm but tactful in turning away those whom the manager does not wish to see. |

## Action

The table on page 14 shows a general identification of the contacts of secretaries inside and outside their organisation.

1. Produce a list of your own contacts in *your* role.

2. List the *expectations* each of these contacts has of you in your secretarial role — their expectations may be in terms of qualities they expect you to have, tasks they expect you to do or behaviour they expect you to display.

3. Identify *how you should behave* to respond to these expectations while maintaining the appropriate support for your manager.

The second part of this exercise may reveal that some contacts have expectations which are unreasonable and go beyond the responsibilities of your secretarial role.

The third part of this exercise may make you stop to consider whether your existing way of responding to these contacts is appropriate or whether you need to change your approach.

Identifying the manager's role and that of the secretary is relatively easy — the difficult part is establishing a partnership which is recognised as a working relationship in which both have equal status but different responsibilities and expertise. The next chapter provides some hints on how to develop this kind of partnership.

# Chapter 2

## Developing the Working Partnership

Developing a working partnership requires effort and commitment from both parties. It is built on mutual respect and understanding. This does not necessarily happen instantly and much of the hard work in creating the relationship must come from the secretary. To be successful in this a combination of knowledge, with practical and interpersonal skill is required.

Obviously, the ideal time at which to determine whether there is a chance of establishing a good relationship with a manager and for setting "the ground rules" is at the interview for a new job.

### Agreeing objectives at a job interview

One of the common mistakes interviewees make is to see the selection interview as a one way interrogation about whether they are suitable for the job. It is therefore important always to remember the aim of a selection interview is:

*A two-way communication exercise to establish that both the manager and job applicant are suited to one another.*

If applicants bear this in mind, they will ensure that, at a job interview, they ask all the questions that will put their minds at rest about whether the organisation is suitable and whether the manager is someone with whom they want to establish a working relationship. On the other hand, it is necessary to avoid being too idealistic and unrealistic in one's expectations.

The checklist below provides some guidelines on finding the right job.

## Guidelines for approaching job interviews

- *Establish objectives*
  Decide what you want from any secretarial job and working relationship. Make a list which you can use as a reference point in the later stages.

- *Check job descriptions carefully*
  Look very carefully at any job description sent with an application form and decide whether the job appears to allow you scope to use your experience, skills and initiative.

- *Produce a list of queries*
  You should note down any aspects of the job description which you do not understand or want to question and make a list of any areas of concern to you which are not mentioned in the job description.

- *Ensure you meet your manager at the interview*
  If your interview is with the personnel department or with an office supervisor, ask to meet the manager — you cannot make important decisions without meeting the person with whom you could be working daily. If this request is refused, think very carefully whether you are prepared to accept secondhand information.

- *Ask about the manager's own job*
  At the interview, find out about the manager's own role within the organisation and what kind of support he or she expects from a secretary.

- *Ask about previous working relationships*
  Find out about the way the manager liked to work with his or
  her previous secretary — how they arranged the working day.

- *Probe any vague answers*
  Just as the interviewer is likely to probe more deeply if you
  provide vague answers to questions, it is your right to probe
  if the interviewer's own answers are ambiguous or vague.

- *Look for signs of "problem" managers*
  Beware of managers who look or sound patronising, dis-
  missive, sexist or too full of their own importance at the
  interview — they are unlikely to change their personality
  after you start work!

- *What about career progression?*
  Do find out about how you can progress within the organisation; in some cases organisations may be prepared to put
  effective secretaries on their management trainee programme; others may indicate that your career depends on
  that of your manager.

- *Give yourself time to make a sound decision.*
  After the interview, assess whether your own objectives and
  those of the manager are compatible. If not, the job is not
  really suitable for you.

# Setting the ground rules

The interview will have provided some information on whether there
is a good chance of the relationship between manager and secretary
being harmonious. However, the first week or two can be a testing time
for how the relationship will develop.

## *Acquiring relevant knowledge*

A person can only be an effective working partner in any relationship when he or she has a good knowledge of the organisation and its business. Therefore one of the first steps is to become familiar with the organisation, department and manager's job.

A good organisation provides all employees with an induction course that is geared to this information; if not, it is necessary to spend every spare moment in the first week researching information.

Useful information and where it can be found is shown in the table below.

## Sources of useful information

| Information | Source |
| --- | --- |
| The organisation's aims and objectives, its range of products and/or services | Memorandum and Articles of Association<br>Annual reports<br>Policy statements<br>Promotional literature<br>Public relations department |
| The company policies, procedures and regulations | Employee handbook<br>Procedure documents and charts<br>Public relations department<br>Personnel department |
| Functions of other departments and sections; key people in the organisation | Talking to other employees<br>Promotional literature<br>Organisation charts<br>Extension lists<br>Employee handbook |
| The work of the manager's department and his or her own job | Becoming familiar with office files<br>Talking to managers and their subordinates |

**Action**

If you lack knowledge in any of the above areas, find out the information now. In addition you can:

(a) read a quality newspaper regularly
(b) visit a library and read articles in relevant magazines about the secretarial role, new office equipment, etc
(c) make a point of reading any in-house magazine produced by your organisation.

## *Agreeing objectives with a manager*

Once a secretary knows how his or her manager's job fits into the overall work of the organisation, he or she is ready for the last point on the table on page 20 — talking to the manager about his or her job and how to provide support.

Many managers are used to secretaries who merely carry out their instructions: "type this letter", "deal with my post", "get this contact on the phone for me", or "take this down to Miss Swift". This requires managers to think about routine aspects of information processing for a major proportion of their day and wastes their managerial time. An efficient secretary can take the initiative in undertaking many of these tasks. However, it does require agreement and a very tactful approach. A sensible way to attempt it is as follows.

## Preparing for the discussion

(a) *State a desire to discuss your future role*
Although it is important for a secretary to show that he or she is "equal but different" early, it is not possible to have a full discussion about how work should or could be divided without some knowledge of the organisation and the work of the section. However, on the first day, you should state your intentions in a firm but friendly manner, eg:

"It is going to take me a little while to find out about the work you do and the work I should be doing. Perhaps once I've found my feet (say, in 10 days' time), we could have a discussion about how I can provide you with the maximum support in your job. In the meantime, I am happy to fit into your previous routine."

(This reveals the speaker to be assertive, likely to have some ideas of his or her own, but also flexible and adaptable.)

(b) *Observe normal office routines*

The intervening time until the discussion can be used to build up an accurate picture of the work of the office. Note any administrative or clerical tasks carried out by your manager which could be undertaken by you. Things to look for are inefficient appointment systems, diary maintenance, handling of post, etc.

(c) *Study the manager as an individual*

What kind of personality does he or she possess? Is he or she likely to welcome ideas or will you have to be extremely tactful and persuasive? At what point in the day is he or she most receptive to sitting down and discussing ideas? What is going to be the cause of any resistance to fresh ideas?

(d) *Record proposals*

Produce a list of proposals based on your information. They should be set out in a format which can be handed to your manager — a short information report might be appropriate (see Chapter 9). Make sure you are familiar with all the information and anticipate the kind of objections your manager might raise to your proposals.

In particular, note how improvements could be made in:

(i)    diary maintenance
(ii)   handling post
(iii)  dealing with correspondence
(iv)   use of bring forward systems
(v)    use of planning aids
(vi)   processing and storing information
(vii)  use of action lists and folders.

(e) *Prepare tactics*

Work out the psychological tactics for your discussion. (A brisk, rather abrupt outline of all the ways the manager's previous secretary might have been inefficient or too servile is not likely to endear your manager to your ideas!)

# Holding the discussion

There are a number of tactics you should employ:

(a) *Recognise your manager's importance*

Play upon his or her need to concentrate on the priority, pro-active aspects of his or her role.

(b) *Present your ideas as proposals*

Do not make it sound as though you are dictating the terms of the partnership. Make suggestions and explain that you would value your manager's views.

(c) *Present your ideas clearly*

Explain your ideas in a direct, concise way with sufficient evidence to back up the proposals you are making (you should have anticipated any objections he or she may raise).

(d) *Listen attentively*

Concentrate demonstrably and show appreciation of your manager's point of view. If you think such arguments need to be countered, then try the assertiveness techniques (mentioned in Chapter 5) to make your point.

(e) *Be prepared to be adaptable*

You are unlikely to get exactly what you want, so it is worth giving way on some items to get the majority accepted — there is always time for another discussion later in your relationship.

(f) *Check agreement on points*

You do not want to find you both had a different interpretation of the discussion at a later date.

Some managers will attempt to tease or cajole their secretaries out of the need for such a meeting. Others will avoid the meeting by never finding time for it to take place. In these circumstances it is necessary to be friendly but insistent that you can only work effectively when you know exactly what your role should be. A typical reply might be:

"I find I can only work really effectively when I know exactly what objectives I should be achieving. Otherwise, I can waste a lot of time doing the wrong tasks efficiently. Don't you agree?"

# Developing the partnership

There are a number of points to bear in mind as you allow your relationship with your manager to develop.

(a) *Don't expect too much too early*

Be tolerant to one another's personality and methods of work (you are both going through a period of great adjustment). Remember that it is normal:

(i)     for managers to compare a new secretary with the previous one

(ii)    for managers to have good and bad days and that stress can make them moody, impatient or even rude

(iii)   to make mistakes at this early stage

(iv)    to find that you both have habits and mannerisms that annoy one another

(v)     that you both may be prone to having your own image of what the "good manager" or "good secretary" should be.

(b) *Encourage regular planning meetings*

Once you have established your role relationship with your manager, ensure that you both adapt as circumstances change by having regular planning meetings. The frequency of the meetings may depend on your manager's role. In some cases it may be a matter of 15 minutes on a given day once a week. For managers who are out of the office frequently, you may need a more flexible arrangement. Such meetings allow for:

(i)     discussion of any future plans that will affect you and your work

(ii)    re-assessment of priorities for the coming week

(iii)    prior warning of potential problems likely to arise in the office

(iv)    suggestions for improving the smooth running of the office.

Note that the idea of a regular meeting is to plan ahead constructively. If there is nothing to discuss, then the meetings should not take place.

(c) *Avoid resentment*

Resentment is one of the most destructive emotions in a working relationship and should be avoided.

(i)    Try to maintain a calm, reasonable approach.

(ii)    If difficulties occur, you should put yourself through some self-analysis. If you consider yourself at fault in any way, think how you can change your behaviour. If you consider your manager is at fault, then have the confidence to take positive action and talk to him or her about it.

(d) *Accept differences in perception*

(i)    There is more than one interpretation of any event, or social situation.

(ii)    Different perceptions to your own are equally valid.

(iii)    Differences in perception occur because of different personalities, motivation and different previous experiences.

There is a traditional exercise which emphasises how people can see things differently. Look at the following picture and write down

what you see. You should see either an old hag with a shawl round her head and a hooked nose, or a pretty young girl with a ribbon round her neck and long eyelashes. *Both are contained within the same picture*. Look again. Can you see the other person?

If your manager's perception of a situation is different to your own, try to understand why this is so and work from there.

(e) *Set a good example* ⠆

People change their attitudes and behaviour slowly. A manager is unlikely to change patterns of behaviour overnight. However, a secretary can set a good example by:

(i) being calmly efficient
(ii) managing time well
(iii) not being susceptible to sudden changes in mood
(iv) showing consideration
(v) showing appreciation of thoughtfulness in others
(vi) showing enthusiasm for the achievements of the manager.

In this way a secretary can gradually "train" a manager into fulfilling his or her responsibilities in the partnership. The Industrial Society has a useful mnemonic for the kind of responsibilities the managerial part of the partnership should assume.

A manager:

**M** makes time to talk
**A** allows the secretary to share in his or her work
**N** never undermines the secretary's role
**A** always plans the day
**G** gives the courtesy the secretary deserves
**E** exit and entry: keeps the secretary informed of his or her movements during the day
**R** recognises that a successful relationship is 50 per cent his or her responsibility.

**Action**

If you are in a working relationship with your present manager which is not totally satisfactory to you, plan how you can bring about changes.

If you are a senior secretary in your organisation who feels underutilised, consider whether you could help your manager by suggesting you become involved in any of the following tasks delegated to you (obviously depending on your individual skills):

- handling your manager's expenses

- organising social events within the department/organisation (eg dinners, sports events, etc)

- running induction training for new secretaries

- representing your manager at some meetings

- making presentations

- doing translations

- designing office layouts

- creating organisation charts

- making contributions to the in-house magazine

- producing notes for speeches, briefing sessions, presentations

- controlling stationery and office equipment.

## The working relationship with your manager

| *Do not* | *Do* |
|---|---|
| ● allow traditional attitudes about secretaries to deter you from achieving the relationship you want | ● think positively about being a secretary |
| ● try to involve your manager in too many routine activities | ● appreciate the nature of and priorities in your manager's role |
| ● underestimate the expertise you possess and can offer in a working partnership | ● recognise the expertise you possess and try to develop a role which *uses* such expertise |
| ● allow technology to make you a servant to the equipment | ● use technology constructively |
| ● allow unreasonable role expectations by others to dictate your behaviour as a secretary | ● decide how you can establish effective role relationships with others |
| ● accept any jobs without consideration of whether you can develop an effective working relationship with the manager | ● approach choosing a job in a logical manner |
| ● put off discussing your working relationship with your manager | ● agree ground rules with your manager for your working relationship |
| ● expect too much too soon in a new relationship | ● make a positive effort to develop the relationship |
| ● allow resentment or differences to sour the relationship — talk things out. | ● set a good example to your manager. |

# Section 2

## Communicating in Face to Face Encounters

### Objectives

By the end of this section you will be able to:

(a) understand the basic communication process and the problems associated with it
(b) appreciate the importance of face to face encounters
(c) apply the basic speaking, listening, and behaving skills in all your face to face encounters
(d) distinguish between submissive, aggressive and assertive behaviour
(e) use some simple assertiveness techniques in your encounters with others inside and outside the organisation
(f) distinguish between different kinds of awkward people and the problems they create
(g) practise some techniques to enable you to handle difficult people effectively
(h) recognise the positive aspects of negotiation as a means of reconciling differences
(i) prepare effectively for a negotiation
(j) conduct a negotiation in a positive, assertive manner.

# Chapter 3

## The Communication Process

It is possible to become adept at laying out and typing memos, letters, reports, tables of statistics or taking down messages from telephone calls — the mechanical routine aspects of "communication" — and yet it is all too easy to forget some of the basic principles which can mean the difference between good and bad communications at work. Therefore, it is worthwhile to look at the basic communication process and recap on the important principles involved in making the process successful.

We can define communication as:

*The transfer of information from one person to another to achieve understanding and bring about action.*

Effective communication within any organisation is vital to its efficiency, its morale and its success. Yet, because we communicate all day, every day, we often fail to think consciously about what makes the transfer of information from one person to another effective. Paradoxically, we are very quick to recognise or draw attention to other people's shortcomings.

"You didn't tell me to do that."
"I can never understand a word he's saying."
"Why don't you say what you mean?"
"The letter the client wrote was so abrupt and rude."

# The importance of communication in the secretarial role

The basic skill behind most other skills needed by a secretary is the ability to communicate by spoken or written word, or by behaviour. It is communication which builds up the trust and confidence between secretary and manager; it helps to deal effectively with visitors, business associates and other managers; it enables the secretary to establish a rapport with other secretaries and it makes him or her approachable to junior staff.

It is necessary to be able to communicate well in order to:

- inform
- persuade
- suggest
- encourage
- consult
- negotiate
- reprimand.

A good communicator will encourage other people to think more carefully about how they communicate — training by example!

This chapter is a reminder about the basic communication process and some of the principles to observe when using it, whether speaking, listening, writing or behaving.

# The communication process

The process can be represented by a simple diagram.

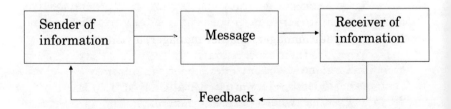

The process is simple enough in theory:

(a) a sender has information which he or she wants to transfer to another person
(b) the idea in the sender's mind is translated into a message and sent to the receiver
(c) the receiver receives the information, understands it and makes the appropriate response
(d) the response indicates to the sender that the message has been received and understood.

Although the process is simple, there are many barriers which can prevent it from working effectively. However, a few basic principles to bear in mind at each stage can help you avoid some of the pitfalls.

## *The sender*

A communication can be ruined by insufficient planning by the sender. Any message starts out as an idea in the mind of the sender. Too often the idea is translated into a message with very little thought. All communication at work requires planning. This may be a few seconds of virtually sub-conscious planning or even several hours of heart-searching thought, depending on the importance of the message and the response which is required.

However long it takes there are basically five or six questions to think about at the planning stage:

(a) *Why communicate?*
— What is the purpose of the message?
— Is it to inform, persuade, etc?
Each purpose will need a different approach in terms of content, language and tone.

(b) *Who is the receiver?*
— Is it your manager, another manager, a visitor, etc?
— What are their expectations?
— What do they already know about the subject?
— What is their relationship/attitude to you?
This will affect the amount of information, the language and tone.

(c) *What should you communicate?*
— What is the actual message to be sent (content)?
— Should you choose written, oral or visual means?
— Should you use a combination of methods?
This will be determined by your answers to "why" and "who".

(d) *How should you communicate?*
— What language should you use?
— What tone would be appropriate?
This will be determined by your answers to "why" and "who".

(e) *When should you communicate?*
— How quickly does the message need to be sent?
— Is there a particular time when the receiver would be more receptive?

and often

(f) *Where should you communicate?*
— Is there a particular place where the receiver may be more responsive to the message?
When and where will be determined by your answers to "why", "what" and "who".

## The message

This really relates to "what" and "how" above.

### The content of the message

There are five basic requirements here. The message should be:

| | | |
|---|---|---|
| (a) *Correct* | — | it should contain information that is accurate. |
| (b) *Complete* | — | it should contain all the information relevant to achieve the purpose. |
| (c) *Clear* | — | the message should be easy to understand and have one meaning only. |
| (d) *Concise* | — | the relevant information should be stated as briefly as possible. |
| (e) *Constructive* | — | the message should be positive so that it creates a favourable response. |

34

## *The method of communicating*

To communicate effectively it is necessary to select the right method or combination of methods. (A reminder of the advantages and limitations of various methods is given in a table on page 36.)

In making a decision consider:

| | | |
|---|---|---|
| (a) *Purpose* | — | the effectiveness of the method in achieving the purpose. |
| (b) *Record* | — | whether or not a permanent record of the message is needed. |
| (c) *Time* | — | how long it takes to transfer the message. |
| (d) *Cost* | — | the cost involved in transferring the message. |
| (e) *Feedback* | — | how quickly feedback from the receiver is required. |

## *The presentation of the message*

Whether speaking or writing, a person can convey information through the way he or she presents the message. Offence can easily be given through ill-chosen words or a tone of voice or style of writing that is in conflict with the content of the message. People can also be annoyed by a badly structured letter or instruction.

The basic rules are shown below.

(a) *Language*

Use simple, direct words, phrases and sentences so that the message is clear. Only use technical jargon if the other person will understand it. Avoid slang expressions.

(b) *Tone*

Approach all receivers, whether in speaking, writing or behaving, in a way that shows respect for their age, authority and attitudes. Never be over familiar or condescending, patronising, servile or vulgar.

(c) *Structure*

Present the information in a sequence that is easy for the receiver to understand. Make the structure logical for the receiver rather than the sender.

## Advantages and limitations of communication media

|  | *Advantages* | *Disadvantages* |
|---|---|---|
| *Written* | There is a permanent record which can be used later for reference.<br><br>It is necessary for contracts and agreements.<br><br>The recipients can take in the message at their own pace.<br><br>It is more accurate for complex or technical information. | Production and delivery of of the message may take time (though electronic mail can reduce this).<br><br>It is a one way method of communication in that feedback is delayed or non-existent. This can mean that misunderstandings are not sorted out immediately.<br><br>It may sometimes be used to avoid facing up to a person. |
| *Oral* | A more personal contact is achieved between sender and receiver.<br><br>Tone, phrasing and (face to face) body language can help to convey the message.<br><br>It is possible to obtain faster feedback. | It is not very good for conveying complex or technical information.<br><br>There is no formal record of the message.<br><br>The recipient can be more easily distracted by noise. |
| *Image* | Image can be used where it is difficult for people to read or hear because of environmental difficulties or disability.<br><br>It is possible to convey information to a mass of people.<br><br>It can overcome language difficulties | There is no control over interpretation of the message or feedback unless it is supported by written or spoken words.<br><br>Personal contact between the sender and receiver is not easy to establish.<br><br>It may require additional skills by the sender and receiver if graphs and diagrams are used. |

## *The receiver*

The purpose of communicating is to bring about some kind of action on the part of the receiver. The word "action" tends to convey the need for physical activity which can be observed (eg a task carried out, an appointment kept, etc).

However, much of our communicating can result in action by the receiver which cannot be directly observed. This may be:

(a) adding to their existing knowledge
(b) confirming or reversing existing beliefs, attitudes or feelings.

There is a tendency to think that the communication process is completed when the message has left the sender — a letter has been sent, a telephone message delivered or an instruction given. We may realise too late that the receiver has misunderstood the message or that it fails to produce the anticipated response.

### *Barriers to effective communication*

There are numerous barriers which prevent messages getting through properly; the fault may lie in the people themselves or in the overall environment and it is important to consider how these barriers can be overcome or reduced by constructive action on the part of the sender or receiver. Some suggestions are given on page 38.

## *Feedback*

A communicator should do his or her utmost to encourage feedback from the receiver to check that the message has achieved its purpose.

Such feedback is secured when we:

(a) receive a reply to a letter or memo
(b) receive a return telephone call
(c) a task is completed
(d) an appointment is kept

or even a nod or an "OK" sign is given.

Feedback is often simpler in face to face or telephone communication because it is possible to see and/or hear whether someone has understood and is likely to respond positively. Where contact is more remote

## Barriers to effective communication and remedies

| Barriers to communication | Remedy by sender | Remedy by receiver |
|---|---|---|
| **PEOPLE** Incomplete, inaccurate information that cannot achieve its purpose. | Sender checks for accuracy and relevance before communicating. | Receiver asks for more or correct information. |
| Poor presentation of the message. | Sender needs to give more thought to language, tone and structure. | Receiver tries to concentrate on content and avoid reacting to tone. |
| An ambiguous message which can have several interpretations. | Sender uses simple, direct words, phrases and sentences. | Receiver does not make assumptions but asks for clarification. |
| Message reaches the receiver at an inappropriate time. | Sender tries to anticipate good and bad times. | Receiver acts on the message as soon as is possible and should notify the sender tactfully if timing is always poor. |
| Hostile attitude of receiver to sender causing unwillingness to act. | If sender is aware of a hostile attitude, try to use neutral language and tone which will not incite hostility. | Receiver should avoid reacting to the person and try to respond to the message. |
| **ENVIRONMENT** Noise which distorts or blocks out the message. | Both senders and receivers should examine their work environments for ways of reducing background noise. | |
| Interruptions which disrupt the message. | Both senders and receivers should ensure that the time and place for important messages reduce the likelihood of frequent interruptions. | |

(such as in written communication) it is necessary to specify clearly the kind of feedback required — when, where, how the sender wants the receiver to respond. This statement on feedback should always occur in the last paragraph of a letter or memo.

# Responsibilities for good communication

Since communication is a two way process, both the sender and the receiver have responsibilities for good communication. These can be summarised as follows.

## *The sender's responsibilities*

These are:

(a) to think about the purpose of the communication before beginning
(b) to think about what to say and how to say it to achieve understanding and a favourable response
(c) to select the most appropriate medium (or combination of media) to achieve the desired purpose
(d) to ensure that the language is suitable for the recipient
(e) to try to eliminate or reduce the barriers to communication
(f) to try to ensure that the message is not likely to be misinterpreted because of inappropriate or poor vocabulary, lack of precision or inappropriate tone
(g) to encourage feedback.

## *The receiver's responsibilities*

These are:

(a) not to be distracted by environmental barriers but to concentrate on the content of the message
(b) not to let personal barriers (own attitude, perceptions, preoccupations) distort the message
(c) to ensure that the message is fully understood; if in doubt, seek clarification rather than risk misinterpretation
(d) to provide the sender with feedback so that he or she knows that the message has been received, understood and acted upon.

# Chapter 4

## Communicating Face to Face

Communicating face to face can be the most satisfying form of communication since it provides the opportunity to:

(a) use the full range of words, tone, facial expressions, eye contact, gestures, posture and touch to convey information
(b) adjust the message according to the response (words, tone, facial expressions, etc)
(c) receive immediate feedback about whether the message is understood and likely to be acted upon.

On the other hand it also poses a threat to good communication in that it is easy to:

(a) speak without thinking
(b) speak without checking that the other person is listening
(c) use tone, facial expressions or gestures which contradict the words of the message, thus creating confusion for the receiver.

Effective communication in a face to face encounter is based on *four* basic skills. These are:

(a) speaking well
(b) listening well
(c) using effective body language
(d) reading body language.

# The importance of good communication in face to face encounters

It will be necessary to use the skills listed above in a whole range of encounters such as:

(a) day to day communication with your manager
(b) receiving visitors
(c) dealing with enquiries or messages from other secretaries or managers
(d) in meetings and at conferences
(e) at business lunches
(f) travelling with your manager.

Whoever your encounter is with you should have a number of objectives. These are:

(a) to deal with the matter in hand efficiently
(b) to leave the other person with a positive impression of you
(c) to say the right thing at the right time in the right way
(d) to feel satisfied with the outcome of the encounter.

This chapter will deal with the four skills listed above, while the next chapter will be devoted entirely to the subject of being assertive. All these skills are necessary to achieve the objectives.

## Speaking well

A secretary needs to be able to speak well whether it is in a relatively informal conversation in the office, participation in a business meeting or a formal oral presentation to a large audience. Your own image and the image of your manager is partly conditioned by the way you speak to other people.

The essential points to remember are:

(a) *Engage brain before opening mouth*

Plan communication — the content and the approach. Think about the points which should be mentioned as well as those which should not (breach of confidence).

(b) *"Switch on" the listener*

Make sure the other person is listening before saying anything important. This can be done by:
   (i)   making a statement of purpose eg "I'd like to talk to you about . . . "
   (ii)  asking a question related to the topic
   (iii) establishing and holding eye contact.

(c) *Speak clearly and audibly*

This means
   (i)   looking at the person while speaking so that the words are projected towards him or her (rather than the desk, the floor, etc)
   (ii)  pronouncing words firmly with clear diction (not mumbling, gabbling or dropping the voice at the end of sentences)
   (iii) adjusting volume to the distance to the other person.

(d) *Use a logical sequence*

Present information in a sequence so that each point follows logically from the one before. This goes back to planning.

(e) *Use appropriate vocabulary*

Adjust vocabulary to the person being addressed; he or she cannot be expected to adjust understanding. For example, within the same department, organisation or specialisation it is common and perfectly acceptable for people to use abbreviations or technical jargon (eg DCF for discounted cash flow; ABTA for the Association of British Travel Agents) but it can be totally bewildering to start using this type of vocabulary with those who are not familiar with it.

(f) *Use simple, direct language*

It is easier to listen and understand a message if it is delivered in short simple sentences using direct uncomplicated words. It is a common failing to use long, convoluted sentences and long words when we are trying to impress. Often, it merely makes it more difficult for the listener to concentrate.

(g) *Use a variety of tone*
   (i)   Allow the tone and pitch of your voice to reflect the words you are saying. If it is exciting news allow the excitement to come through in your voice; when conveying bad news allow sympathy to come through.
   (ii)   Avoid a monotone (every word pronounced exactly the same without any variation or emotion) — it will send people to sleep.
   (iii)   At all costs, avoid sounding condescending, patronising, over familiar, grovelling or fawning.

# Listening well

Every secretary needs to be a good listener — it is an implicit part of the partnership agreement. Managers often want to talk through their plans or require a sympathetic ear for their problems (work or personal); clients and visitors expect an interested and lively response to their conversation; other secretaries expect to be able to discuss their successes and failures, etc.

In a work situation, being a good listener helps towards personal efficiency in that it enables the receivers to:

(a) act on instructions quickly and accurately
(b) pick up good ideas from other people
(c) find out about other people's attitudes towards them and their work
(d) avoid giving offence or embarrassment by having to ask people to repeat information.

## Barriers to effective listening

There are a number of barriers which can affect the ability of receivers to listen well. These are:

(a) making the assumption that hearing is the same as listening

(b) allowing aspects about the appearance, voice or mannerisms of the speaker to distract the receiver from the message

(c) allowing aspects of the work environment to disturb the receiver's concentration (noise, people, etc)

(d) missing behavioral messages (see next section)

(e) allowing negative attitudes about the speaker to block concentration

(f) trying to do two things at once.

By being aware of the barriers it is possible to

(a) improve one's own listening skills

(b) help the listener to concentrate on one's own spoken messages.

---

### Action

Try to help other people's listening skills by thinking critically about the following questions:

— Do you always "switch on" the listener to your message?

— Do you have any distracting gestures or mannerisms that you use when speaking?

— Do you create a suitable environment for your listener to concentrate?

— Do you use body language which reinforces your words?

— Do you take trouble to create positive attitudes towards you?

---

## Improving your own listening skills

There are a number of techniques you can use to improve your own listening skills.

(a) *Think of listening as an active process*
This means giving the message your whole attention — brain as well as ears!

(b) *Focus on the speaker*

Maintain good eye contact with the speaker. This aids concentration, establishes a rapport and enables you to pick up non-verbal messages.

(c) *Pick out important parts of the message*

Listen for key phrases, stressed words, repeated phrases or pauses used to create emphasis.

(d) *Take notes*

If the message is important, complex or long, be prepared to write brief notes. Do not trust your memory.

(e) *Ask questions*

If you do not understand a message or think you may have misinterpreted it, ask questions and clarify the key points. It is better to be embarrassed at this stage than make a crucial mistake later.

(f) *Ignore distractions*

Remind yourself to block out distractions which come from the speaker or from the environment in which the exchange is taking place.

(g) *Encourage the speaker*

If the speaker is having difficulty explaining the message, help out by asking questions rather than letting him or her struggle.

(h) *Demonstrate attention*

During long explanations, use a number of techniques which demonstrate that you are concentrating on listening:

(i)    have an alert, interested expression on your face. Do not let it lapse into looking bored, pre-occupied or indulgent

(ii)    lean very slightly forward towards the speaker

(iii)    use facial expressions, gestures, short phrases or noises to respond to the speaker and show your attention (eg looking surprised, nodding agreement, using "Mm", "Uh huh", "Really!").

# Using body language effectively

Although getting the spoken message right is important in good face to face communication, listeners derive only about 10 per cent of their understanding of the message from the actual words. 90 per cent comes from non-verbal communication including:

(a) *How we say the words* — tone, speed, pitch, etc
(b) *How we behave* — facial expression, eye contact and movement, gestures, posture, touch and proximity.

If there is conflict or contradiction between what is said and how the speaker presents the information, receivers place greater reliance on the non-verbal communication.

This means that how a person behaves — body language — is a very important part of effective communication.

## *The importance of overall appearance*

Obviously the overall appearance of any secretary is important. The total image, in terms of dress, hair or grooming that is presented to other people, particularly those outside the organisation, affects their perception not only of him or her but of his or her manager and even the employing organisation. A clean, neat, well-groomed and confident secretary will convey an image of an efficient, organised office and employer. However, using body language well goes beyond overall appearance; it requires a conscious use of a wide range of features to convey a specific message at a particular time.

## *The nature of body language*

It is useful to think of body language like the spoken language. It has the equivalent of:

(a) words — an individual facial expression or gesture
(b) groups of words in sentences — a combination of expression, gesture, posture, etc.

Just as it is not possible to convey a message well by linking odd words together, so it is not possible to use body language effectively until the right combination is found. There are other analogies too. In spoken language people may sometimes attempt to communicate by opening their mouths and just letting the words come out without prior thought (then they wonder why the receiver gets the wrong message). In body language too, people can give out sub-conscious signals through gestures and expressions — messages not intended to be conveyed to the receiver.

It is therefore important:

(a) to know the message that certain body signals convey to a receiver
(b) to use body language *consciously* in order to reinforce positively what you want to say.

Although this section will go through individual signals, remember that you actually use them in *clusters* and it is the total cluster which conveys the full message to the receiver. You therefore need to consider how to use combinations of signals.

## *Forms of body language*

### *Eye contact*

This relates to the level of actual eye contact between the sender and receiver.

| *Characteristic* | | *Possible message* |
|---|---|---|
| ● Fixed, staring eye | conveys | rudeness or a challenge |
| ● Occasional furtive glances at the receiver | conveys | nervousness or lack of confidence |
| ● Prolonged lack of eye contact | conveys | disinterest, insolence or an intention to deceive |

## *Eye size and movement*

| *Characteristic* | | *Possible message* |
|---|---|---|
| • Narrowing eyes | conveys | questioning or doubt |
| • Opening eyes wide | conveys | innocence or vulnerability |

## *Facial expressions*

Many English people tend to have rather immobile faces when put into semi-formal situations (the "stiff upper lip"). Those whose jobs involve presentation to others (interviewers, negotiators, television presenters, actors, teachers) are often trained to use more mobile facial expressions to show a range of thoughts and feelings.

A secretary's job involves a great deal of contact with others and if you can use facial expression to reinforce words of:

- sympathy
- amusement
- anxiety
- doubt
- confidence or
- urgency,

etc it will enhance your own communication. To see the range of which you are capable, just watch people holding a relaxed conversation among friends. You will see that they use:

- the set of the mouth
- the angle of the chin
- the position of the eyebrows
- the nose

as well as their eyes to show this range of feelings.

## *Gestures*

The main instruments for gestures are the hands. Some people use their hands a great deal when talking; others keep them relatively still.

It is often the position of the hands and arms that give the most marked signals. For example:

| Characteristic | | Possible message |
|---|---|---|
| ● Tightly folded arms across the body | convey | defensiveness<br>a desire to set up a barrier<br>an unwillingness to share opinions |
| ● Using a wagging or slicing finger to make a point | conveys | aggressiveness<br>a desire to impose an opinion on others |
| ● Clasping hands together and showing white knuckles towards the receiver | conveys | repressed aggression or resentment or repressed anxiety |
| ● Fiddling with jewellery, face, hair or clothes | conveys | nervousness or a desire to hide the truth |
| ● Showing an open palm to the receiver when making a point | conveys | honesty or integrity |

## Handshakes

There are several kinds of handshake and they all convey different messages.

| Characteristic | | Possible message |
|---|---|---|
| ● A limp wristed handshake or allowing someone to twist your hand underneath | conveys | submissiveness |
| ● Keeping your hand on top of the other's or grasping his or her elbow at the same time | conveys | dominance |
| ● A firm, straight handshake | conveys | equality<br>friendliness |

### Stance

| Characteristic | | Possible message |
|---|---|---|
| • Slouching or stooping | conveys | reluctance or lack of confidence |
| • Standing on one foot or shifting from one foot to the other or twisting feet round one another | conveys | nervousness |

### Sitting posture

| Characteristic | | Possible message |
|---|---|---|
| • Rounded and hunched shoulders | conveys | nervousness or servility |
| • Leaning back in chair with hands clasped behind head | conveys | casualness, or over-confidence or superiority |
| • Elbow on desk, head on hand | conveys | boredom or interest depending on how heavily the head leans on the hand and the amount of eye contact |
| • Sitting upright and leaning slightly forward | conveys | interest |

## Proximity and territory

We all have our own territory — our bedroom, our chair, our office. We also have a need for personal space — a sub-consciously recognised area around us that we consider our own. We do not like our personal space to be invaded uninvited and become nervous and resentful when this happens.

We also convey information to others by the degree of space we maintain between ourselves and them.

| Characteristic | | Possible message |
|---|---|---|
| • A large space between two people | conveys | formality, caution or dislike |
| • A narrow space between two people | conveys | informality, trust or liking |

If someone oversteps the personal space which another sees as appropriate to the situation, he or she becomes anxious and defensive and is likely to start giving out nervous body language signals and may even back off physically.

| Characteristic | | Possible message |
|---|---|---|
| • Standing talking to a person when he or she is sitting | conveys | authority or desire to dominate |
| • Talking to someone across a desk or table (a barrier) | conveys | formality defensiveness |
| • Removing the barrier and sitting at 45° to one another or sitting at a round table | conveys | informality a desire to be friendly |

# Interpreting body language

## Conflict between words and body language

The section above provides some idea of how the signals given out by body language may be interpreted. Most people interpret body language as a subconscious process. For example, have you ever commented to your manager or another secretary: "I don't like that person" or "My intuition tells me that he isn't telling us the complete story"?

That was your subconscious interpretation of body language working. The signals you were receiving from expression, gesture, stance, etc were contradicting the words to which you were listening.

**Example**

A manager approaches you for some information and says:

"Your manager said it would be OK for you to give the information to me."

While saying the words he is fingering the inside of his collar, shifting from foot to foot and avoiding eye contact.

It is very likely you would mistrust the words.

To be a good listener it is necessary to watch body language signals consciously and use them in conjunction with spoken words. If there is a conflict between the two, it is often safer to depend on what the body language is saying. However, do take note of the next point.

## *Interpreting body language clusters*

Remember that it is necessary to look at clusters of body language signals, not individual signals in isolation. Most individual signals can have more than one interpretation, eg folded arms can indicate that the person is:

(a) cold
(b) feels threatened
(c) feels resentful.

Here are some examples of common clusters:

**Examples**

Message — "I'm listening to you."

- Good eye contact

- Leaning slightly forward

- Nodding agreement from time to time

Message — "I want to ignore you."
- Avoids eye contact by looking down
- Hand on forehead
- Frowning
- Barrier erected by the hand, arms or use of furniture

Message — "I want to interrupt you."
- Fiddling with hair or clothes
- Restless posture
- Staring intensely
- Touching your arm

Message — "I'm more important than you."
- Casual posture whether standing or in chair (eg leaning back in chair, hands behind head or leg over the arm of the chair)
- Looking at ceiling
- Using finger to make points
- Emphasising own height
- Using status symbols
- Putting fingers together in the form of a steeple

Message — "I feel resentful about what you are saying."
- Folded arms and/or crossed legs
- Avoidance of eye contact
- Frowning

Message — "I feel angry about what you are saying."
- Folded arms or hands gripped tightly together
- Very strong eye contact
- Frowning
- Heightened colour

**Action**

A good way to develop your body language skills is to select any kind of interactive programme on the television — chat show, interview, live audience participation programme, etc and then turn off the sound for five minutes.

See how much of the message you can pick up by simply observing non-verbal communication.

If you repeat the experiment daily for a period of a week or two, you will be amazed how much more observant you can become.

## *Consider cultural differences*

When interpreting gestures consciously used by people in other countries, do remember that some have completely different meanings.

For example, in some eastern mediterranean countries the sign we use with thumb and forefinger for the OK sign is a rude gesture! Some remote tribes shake their heads to signal agreement. Some nationalities believe in much less personal space and more proximity than we do.

Therefore, interpret body language cautiously when travelling abroad.

# Ways of upsetting other people in face to face encounters

There are many ways in which it is possible to upset other people, particularly those outside one's own organisation. It is possible for receptionists and secretaries as well as managers to make visitors feel:

- unwelcome
- annoyed
- intrusive
- embarrassed
- uncomfortable.

55

This is often associated with:

(a) looking:
    (i)    uninterested in them or their business
    (ii)   bored or apathetic
    (iii)  cross
    (iv)  untidy
    (v)   disorganised
(b) sounding
    (i)    aggressive or rude
    (ii)   too submissive or uncertain
    (iii)  unco-operative
    (iv)  sarcastic
    (v)   patronising
(c) behaving badly by
    (i)    leaving them alone for too long
    (ii)   turning one's back on them
    (iii)  chatting to other employees about seemingly trivial matters in front of them.

It is possible to create a positive image by always:

(a) acknowledging people's presence immediately
(b) apologising if it is not possible to talk to them immediately (ie because of being already involved elsewhere); however, conclude the other conversation as quickly as possible
(c) looking tidy and efficient
(d) using welcoming and positive body language
(e) speaking clearly and audibly
(f) using a tone which conveys courtesy, interest and lively concern
(g) listening carefully and attentively
(h) giving accurate, clear information
(i) trying to help visitors and outside contacts whether it is one's responsibility or not. Take the initiative in approaching anyone who looks lost, confused or in need of assistance.

## The basic stages of any encounter

You are probably quite adept at talking with other secretaries informally or chatting briefly to visitors before an appointment with your manager. However, there are occasions when your responsibility for a successful encounter may go beyond a simple conversation. For example, you may have to:

(a) receive representatives or technical engineers from office or computer equipment firms to discuss your office needs
(b) undertake a formal meeting with another manager, one of your manager's subordinates, a customer, client, etc on behalf of your manager.

Whether an encounter is formal or informal, there are four basic stages; it is easy to remember these as WASP:

**W** welcome
**A** ask questions
**S** supply information
**P** part.

Some points to bear in mind at each of these stages follow.

## *Welcome*

When the meeting is on your territory, you should initiate the welcome. The basic message of welcome is:

(a) to acknowledge the other's presence immediately by establishing firm eye contact and smiling
(b) if you are talking to someone else, excuse yourself and concentrate on your visitor
(c) if you are some distance away, move towards him or her and extend your hand for a firm handshake
(d) introduce yourself (and your position in the organisation if necessary)
(e) ask a simple question to start the conversation.

## *Acquire information*

This means asking questions. There are several points to bear in mind.

(a) Ask the right kind of questions:
  (i)  closed questions (those requiring brief yes or no answers) to confirm facts
  (ii) open questions (starting with why, what, how, etc) to secure details or probe reasons.
(b) Listen to other people's answers attentively and interpret their body language.
(c) Demonstrate attention by using "Umm", "I see", etc and by using appropriate attention-giving body language.
(d) Makes notes of the most important points so that you have a record.

## Supply information

(a) Have all the relevant facts to hand, preferably in note form rather than in your head.
(b) Apply the basic principles of speaking well.
(c) Break up the information into meaningful "chunks" which are easy for the other person to absorb.
(d) Consciously use body language to reinforce the words and encourage the other person into a positive response.

## Part

(a) In more formal situations, summarise what has been discussed or decided.
(b) Check whether any further action is required. If so, agree
  (i)   what that action is,
  (ii)  who is taking the action,
  (iii) any deadlines for the action.
(c) Thank the other person for his or her time and say goodbye.

These basic points apply to all face to face encounters. However, it is one thing to recognise what you should do and quite another to apply these points with confidence. The next chapter will introduce you to some assertiveness techniques which you can use to make your encounters more satisfying for all concerned.

# Chapter 5

## Assertiveness Techniques

A valuable asset for a successful secretary is to be assertive. Unfortunately, many people equate the word "assertive" with being dominant or aggressive. This is not its true meaning. Because of this confusion over the two words some people prefer to call assertiveness "self-confidence". If your skills and qualities as a secretary or administrative assistant are to be recognised and appreciated by other people and if you are to feel an equal with your manager, then confidence is essential.

If you appear too submissive or accommodating, those who are aggressive and rude will delight in bullying you, flaunting their authority and encroaching on your personal space; this will do nothing for your self-image or your reputation as a secretary.

If you appear aggressive or domineering yourself, you may be able to "throw your weight about" with submissive people but you will be constantly having confrontations with other aggressive people and you are likely to be disliked and avoided.

### Importance of being assertive

If you are assertive you will find that:

(a) it helps you to deal with difficult managers and visitors
(b) it enables you to secure co-operation from other people more easily — from your manager, other managers, other secretaries, clerks;

(c) it helps you to state your opinions or say how you feel when you think this is important, ie in formal and informal meetings

(d) it avoids being "taken advantage of" or "put upon" by others (eg other managers or secretaries wanting favours)

(e) it avoids accepting blame for something you have not done (eg in personal complaints/criticism)

(f) it makes you feel better about yourself and your behaviour.

# Recognising the differences in submissive, aggressive and assertive behaviour

## *Submissive behaviour*

There are some definite signs you can detect of submissive behaviour. Submissive people:

(a) do not express how they feel (except to close friends)

(b) are imposed upon with tasks that they do not want to do or ought not to be doing

(c) avoid confronting people because they do not want to upset or anger them

(d) believe in "anything for a quiet life"

(e) prefer to makes excuses than give reasons that may offend

(f) go along with the decisions of the majority even when they disagree with them

(g) often feel frustrated, unhappy, hurt or anxious.

The submissive person:

(a) sounds hesitant

(b) uses a very quiet voice

(c) stumbles over words

(d) prefixes many sentences with "I'm afraid" or "I'm sorry"

(e) allows sentences to trail off into silence.

The submissive person's body language is:

(a) hunched shoulders

(b) crossed arms (for protection)

(c) nervous or clumsy gestures (eg fiddling with hair, clothes or jewellery)

(d) avoidance of eye contact

(e) anxious facial expressions

(f) maintaining an exaggerated distance from other people

(g) a limp handshake.

## *Aggressive behaviour*

Aggressive people:

(a) speak their minds, even if it upsets others or gives offence

(b) believe in being blunt and to the point

(c) believe attack is the best form of defence

(d) easily lose their tempers

(e) complain very readily

(f) do not believe in apologising (even if they are in the wrong)

(g) often feel defensive, hostile or angry.

They sound:

(a) loud

(b) strident

(c) cross or rude

and often

(d) speak fast or with deliberate slowness

(e) use negative words or phrases, eg "no", "can't", "it's impossible"

(f) use the word "I".

Their body language is:

(a) folded arms

(b) clenched hands

(c) jabbing or slicing fingers

(d) standing when others are sitting

(e) leaning over people or encroaching on their space

(f) fixed, staring eye contact

(g) a firm jaw line and jutting chin

(h) placing their hand on top in a handshake.

## *Assertive behaviour*

Assertive people:

(a) express their feelings openly to others but with consideration for them

(b) are able to see and acknowledge the other person's point of view

(c) can keep their emotions under control

(d) deal with problems rather than avoiding them or creating conflict

(e) try to resolve differences with others by discussing them openly and reaching common agreement

(f) feel confident and good about themselves.

They:

(a) sound calm

(b) have a firm, clear, steady voice

(c) use language which shows they are listening

(d) ask questions to find out other's needs or points of view

(e) avoid words which incite conflict.

Their body language is:

(a) frequent eye contact

(b) relaxed but upright posture

(c) open palm gestures

(d) a range of body language which helps to express feelings and show concern

(e) a firm, straight handshake.

# Range of behaviour

Having read through the above characteristics, you will probably realise that you may have exhibited all three forms of behaviour — it all depends on where you are and who you are with. This is true of most people.

**Action**

Try to identify one situation in which you have behaved submissively and one in which you have behaved aggressively.

Think about the way you behaved and the words you used.

How did you feel after the encounter was over?

Often aggressive behaviour can leave a feeling of self-satisfaction — a feeling of winning. However, there is usually a reaction later since aggressive behaviour creates resentment and a "revenge" psychology in others. Submissive behaviour makes people feel resentful and guilty. They feel they should have been able to express themselves more clearly or stand up for their rights more strongly. We all need to work towards trying to be assertive in our behaviour in most of our encounters socially and at work. It is the best pattern of behaviour for feeling good about oneself and relating well to other people.

Assertiveness is partly an attitude of mind and partly the application of some simple basic techniques.

# Moving towards being more assertive

## *Self-analysis*

The first step is to be honest about your assertiveness problems. You need to think hard about the situations which, or people who, create assertiveness problems for you. In general, people are more concerned about being assertive when they see themselves as too submissive. Some typical problem situations mentioned by other secretaries are:

(a) "meeting new people for the first time"
(b) "stating my dissatisfactions at work to my manager"
(c) "being pushed around or manipulated by dominant people, particularly other managers who have no real authority over my work"
(d) "trying to ask someone to do me a favour or give me help"
(e) "being able to say 'no' when I think I should"

(f) "speaking up and asking questions in a meeting, particularly where there are people who are superior in authority"

(g) "disagreeing with someone who is very domineering".

You may have others.

---

**Action**

Make a list of the situations that you find difficult. You may find some specific help in the sections below.

---

## Make a commitment to more assertive behaviour

As with diets or giving up smoking, it is only possible to succeed by having a strong commitment to the project. You must be able to see positive benefits to yourself in more assertive behaviour.

Some typical benefits of being assertive are:

(a) you feel better about yourself

(b) you recognise you are responsible for your own feelings and behaviour and tend not to makes excuses or blame others

(c) you waste less time and energy worrying about your status in the eyes of other people

(d) your value as an employee and as a person is more likely to be recognised by others.

---

**Action**

Make a personal list of the benefits to you, as an individual and as an employee, of being more assertive.

---

## Accept the concept of mutual rights

If you go back to the characteristics of assertive behaviour you will see that being assertive is not just speaking out for what you want and how you feel; it is also accepting that other people have the same rights (the concept of mutual rights).

If you know you are bad at doing this, it is a good idea to put up a notice in your office which reminds you (and others). Your manager and others may think it a bit of a joke at first but persevere — it does help you to remember what you want to achieve. It can be something similar to the following:

---

### My Bill of Rights

I, the undersigned, have the right to:

- be treated with respect
- have and express my own feelings and opinions
- be listened to and be taken seriously
- say NO without feeling guilty
- ask for what I want
- ask for information
- make mistakes
- choose not to assert myself

and I will accord others the same rights.

Signed _____

---

## *A standard procedure for encounters requiring assertiveness*

(a) Listen attentively to what the other person has to say.
(b) Show by words and body language that you understand the other person's position.
(c) State your thoughts calmly and with control.
(d) State what you want to happen.
(e) Recognise that often a compromise between two positions is necessary.

This means developing an assertiveness vocabulary that avoids the harshness of the aggressive person as well as the apologetic hesitance of the submissive person.

Some examples of suitable vocabulary are show below.

## Examples of assertive vocabulary

(a) *Showing understanding* can come through in phrases such as:

- "I can see you are . . ."
- "I can see your point/case . . ."
- "I understand your position . . ."
- "I appreciate . . ."
- "I can see why you think . . ."

(b) *Stating how you feel* can come through phrases such as:

- "I feel . . ."
- "I think . . ."
- "I believe . . ."

(c) *Stating what you want to happen* can seem dominant if made as a brash statement. Assertive people often phrase their ideas as logical suggestions which are in the interest of both parties, eg

- "Would you agree?"
- "Would that help?"
- "What do you think?"
- "How do you respond to this suggestion?"

You can *link understanding their position to your's* with linking words. Good linking words are:

- "however"
- "alternatively"
- "nevertheless".

Avoid using "but"; it is a short, rather harsh word which indicates that someone is taking a totally opposite view!

For example, to your manager:

> "I can appreciate that it is important for you to have this report completed today; however, I feel upset that you should expect me to work late tonight at such short notice. I have an appointment which I must keep. I don't mind working through my lunchtime though. Would that help you?"

## *Practise assertive body language*

If you are to look and sound assertive, remember to speak:

(a) in a firm, clear voice
(b) at a steady pace
(c) maintaining good eye contact
(d) maintaining an upright position but leaning slightly towards the person
(e) using facial expressions and gestures which support the words you are using.

# Dealing with problem situations

The rest of this chapter will help you deal with some of the situations quoted earlier that have given secretaries problems.

## *Asking someone to do something or asking for a favour*

Your worst problem here is that:

(a) you are frightened of a rejection and therefore you are likely to be tempted to present your request in such a submissive way that it makes rejection easy. You may unwittingly do this by hovering near the person, not meeting their eyes and speaking hesitantly, eg "Er . . . I know this is imposing on you, but . . . could you possibly . . ." This invites the response: "That's right — it is imposing on me."
(b) you present it in such an unpleasant, domineering way that the other person does not want to co-operate. For example, leaning

over someone, glaring at them and saying in an angry voice, "You have to do it if I say so" can provoke the response, "No I don't."

The best approach is:

(a) to state your request very clearly
(b) to use simple, direct language
(c) to maintain good eye contact throughout
(d) to smile
(e) to use a pleasant tone.

It is far more difficult to refuse someone using these techniques!

## Saying "no"

Despite what has been said above, at times it is necessary to say "no" to other people. It is important that you do learn to say no because if you are conned or bullied into saying "yes" you are not committed to the task and probably have very little motivation towards doing it well. In many cases, the other person would prefer to have an honest "no" than a grudging compliance. Use an approach similar to the one stated on page 67 about working late.

If people persist, then the "fogging" technique can sometimes help. Fogging is creating confusion for the person by agreeing with part of what they said.

### An example of fogging technique

In the case about working late, if your manager had accused you of being selfish, you might say:

"Yes, you may be right that I am being self-centred in putting my appointment first; nevertheless I still am not prepared to cancel it at such short notice."

## Taking criticism

This is difficult for everyone. If someone criticises your work, your appearance or your behaviour there is a tendency to become resentful and defend yourself vehemently or else become over-apologetic. Avoid reacting emotionally to a criticism.

The best approach is to:

(a) listen to the criticism and show understanding of the point that is being made
(b) agree with any truth in the criticism or agree with the logic of the argument — do not waste time with excuses
(c) allow for improvement
(d) ask for specific examples of the behaviour, if the criticism is too generalised or there is little or no truth in it
(e) explain calmly how you feel, if the criticism is delivered in an unpleasant destructive way.

### An example of handling criticism

For example, your manager complains about some errors in calculations in a report you produced and you are tempted to feel resentful because it is most unusual for you to make mistakes and she had asked you to do the report at short notice.

It is a waste of your time and emotions to argue whether it is fair for her to criticise you for a "one off" situation or to blame her for creating the pressure which resulted in the mistakes. So:

"Yes, what you are saying is true; I did make some errors in the report and I appreciate that this can create a bad image. I don't like producing work with errors and I will certainly do all I can to ensure it doesn't happen again. However, I feel we could avoid any repetition of this if we sat down for five minutes to discuss priorities in the present workload so that I can give sufficient attention to important work. What do you think?"

This depersonalises the situation, does not involve blame being passed backwards and forwards, and attempts to prevent the same kind of situation occurring again.

## *Standing up for yourself*

When it is a case of someone else attempting to impose his or her views on you, it is a good idea to try to anticipate the view that he or she is about to put forward and then agree with it (fogging).

"Yes, I agree that . . . however, my point is that . . .".

### An example of making someone listen to you

---

If a visitor persists in trying to see your manager you could try:

*You*    "Mr Wallis can't see you today, Mr Caldwell. His appointment book is full.

*Visitor*    "Go on. He'll see me".

*You*    "Mr Wallis has the rule that he cannot see people without an appointment. Can I make you an appointment for later in the week?"

*Visitor*    "But I've come some distance. I'm sure he'll make an exception in my case."

*You*    "I'm afraid not, Mr Caldwell. I can make you an appointment on Thursday."

*Visitor*    "But you can squeeze me in this afternoon, can't you?"

*You*    "Mr Wallis insists on seeing visitors by appointment. Would you like me to pencil you in for 2.30 pm on Thursday?"

You will need to repeat the message until the person ultimately listens.

---

# The power of positive thought

Part of assertiveness is positive thinking, believing that it is possible to handle situations assertively. However, there are moments of doubt in all of us — about the very tricky meeting or the particularly unpleasant individual. It is these situations which penetrate our thoughts and have us imagining all the things that could possibly go wrong.

At these times, don't allow those negative thoughts to persist. Think positively. Remind yourself of your rights, the techniques you can try, the preparation for the encounter that you have made and tell yourself that you can handle it.

There is no guarantee that assertiveness is going to mean that encounters turn out as you want them to every time. Sometimes you will be assertive and still fail to achieve your objectives. However, even in these times of failure, you should still come away from an encounter feeling happier about yourself and your behaviour.

Some of the people who may really test your assertiveness are identified in the next chapter.

# Chapter 6

## Dealing with Difficult People

Now that you have covered the basic principles of oral communication, body language and assertiveness, you are ready to handle most interpersonal relationships. This chapter will help you with the really tricky situations, particularly those which involve being on the receiving end of complaints or having to deal with any of the following types of people:

(a) the person whose temper flares easily
(b) the consistently rude, sarcastic person
(c) the talkative type
(d) the supercilious, superior type who knows better than you
(e) the persistent questioner who will never accept your information
(f) the silent type who will not communicate with you.

Each person has a dread of particular types of personality and they may be encountered:

  (a) in reception
  (b) in the office
  (c) at a business lunch
  (d) while travelling.

When you do encounter one of these individuals, the temptation is to let your emotional reactions take over, yet it is important that you remember your assertiveness and basic communication skills. Emotional control is particularly important in a secretary. Often you hold confidential information about your manager's business and you may be persuaded to blurt out some privileged information if you lose control.

# Why people create difficulties

Each type of problem person creates his or her own kind of difficulty for the secretary who is trying to deal with him or her. The table opposite identifies the kind of difficulties each type may cause.

# Some basic principles for handling difficult people

## *Recognise the reactions they arouse*

Difficult people often bring out the worst in us. If someone is being rude, it is hard to remain calm and deal with him or her politely and efficiently. It is important that your image and that of your manager and company remains intact however difficult the other person makes it.

The first stage in controlling emotions is to accept the reactions they are likely to arouse in you. We have listed some common reactions on page 76.

## *Try to understand the reason for their behaviour*

When other people's attitudes and behaviour create difficulties in handling them, we all tend merely to dismiss them as unpleasant people. It is worth thinking more deeply than this.

## Types of difficult people

| Types of person | Why the behaviour creates difficulties |
|---|---|
| Angry | They direct their anger, whatever the cause, at you. |
| | They show anger by becoming loud, strident, banging tables, pointing fingers. |
| Rude | They are rude and sarcastic however much you try to help them. |
| | They will find fault whatever action you take. |
| | They show rudeness by attacking your attitudes and actions with sarcasm. |
| Talkative | They talk non-stop and wander off the point. |
| | It is difficult to break into their monologue because they talk louder or more rapidly if you try to interrupt. |
| | They often disrupt more important work or create queues. |
| Superior | They belittle your ideas, opinions or information, or ignore them. |
| | They often talk loudly so that they can "show off" their superior knowledge to other people. |
| | Their approach is accompanied by challenging superior body language. |
| Persistent questioner | They disregard information and consequently require it to be repeated several times. |
| | They often question your authority or ability to deal with them. |
| | They often gloat if they can find a gap in your knowledge. |
| Silent | They expect you to use telepathy to understand their needs. |
| | It is difficult to initiate a conversation with them. |
| | Their monosyllabic answers to questions protract the encounter. |

## Common reactions to difficult people

| Type | Common reaction |
| --- | --- |
| Angry person | Retaliate in kind. |
| | Be intimidated and give way to them. |
| | Become flustered and disorganised. |
| | Say or do things you may regret later. |
| Rude person | Similar to above. |
| Talkative person | Become curt and rude. |
| | Be discourteous by showing boredom. |
| | Try to pass them on to someone else. |
| Superior person | Become annoyed, exasperated. |
| | Begin to doubt your own information. |
| | They succeed in making you feel inferior (guilt and resentment). |
| Persistent questioner | Become resentful. |
| | Feel humiliated. |
| | Be tempted to use a "take it or leave it" attitude. |
| Silent | Become exasperated. |
| | Give up trying to help. |

## Reflection

Have you been angry or rude to someone else?

Have you ever been guilty of being over-talkative?

Have you ever shown your mistrust of someone's ability/authority to help you?

Have you given way to the temptation to demonstrate your superiority?

Have you ever been rather reticent to talk to someone?

If so, why?

## Possible reasons for "difficult" behaviour

| Type | Possible explanation of behaviour |
|---|---|
| Angry person | No-one has attempted to resolve the problem.<br><br>Getting worked up is the only way he or she can voice a complaint or stand up for himself or herself. |
| Rude person | No excuse! |
| Talkative person | It is a nervous reaction to a problem situation.<br><br>Lonely.<br><br>Naturally extrovert. |
| Superior person | Proud of newly acquired knowledge.<br><br>Needs admiration and flattery.<br><br>Wants to preserve differences in authority or status. |
| Persistent questioner | Needs frequent reassurance.<br><br>May be faced with an even more difficult person who is putting pressure on him or her for accurate information.<br><br>May think you look rather young to know very much about the topic. |
| Silent person | Submissive type.<br><br>Worried about committing himself or herself by responding too easily.<br><br>Does not like being pressurised into making a decision. |

The answer to the questions in the reflective activity is probably "Yes" and no doubt you had good reasons for this behaviour — you did not perceive yourself to be an unpleasant, difficult person.

Whenever you encounter difficult people it is worth considering whether there is any justification for their approach; try to see the situation from their point of view. Some possible reasons are given on page 77.

## General procedure for handling difficult people

There is a simple procedure to follow for handling most difficult types of people. It is:

(a) *Stay calm*

You cannot hope to deal with them in a business-like way unless you remain in control of your own emotions.

(b) *Listen*

If you are to handle them effectively you need to find out what they want and what they expect of you. Part of their difficult behaviour may stem from the fact that they are frustrated that no-one has really listened to them.

(c) *Use your professional knowledge*

You can find out more about their needs and help them to provide facts or express requests by asking them appropriate closed or open questions.

(d) *Do not take their behaviour personally*

Resist the emotional reactions shown on page 76. Instead, remember that they are reacting to the situation by "getting at you". If you remember this, you can remove yourself from the full impact of their words and behaviour and get on with dealing with the problem or complaint, etc.

(e) *Get on with whatever action is needed*

The quickest way to deal with a difficult person is to get on with whatever action is needed in the situation — provide the information required, take steps to resolve the problem, get him or her to the destination on time. It may not turn all difficult people into pleasant, amenable types but it does show efficiency and gets them "out of your hair" as quickly as possible.

## Techniques for handling difficult people

| *Type* | *Technique* |
|---|---|
| Angry | • Allow them to let off steam (you cannot help them until they have expressed their emotion).<br>• Apologise briefly for any inconvenience caused to them.<br>• Steer the conversation from emotional reactions about past or present events towards positive action for the future.<br>• Allow facial expressions to show genuine helpfulness.<br>• Get on with putting the matter right (after all, that is what they want!). |
| Rude | • Stay calm.<br>• Do not take the rudeness personally — he or she is probably like that to everyone!<br>• Keep smiling.<br>• Allow facial expressions to show genuine helpfulness.<br>• Get on with what you need to do — it is the best way of getting rid of them! |
| Talkative | • Use brief gaps in the monologue to pick on key words and use these to move forward the action needed.<br>• Address the person by name; it generally causes a brief lull in the monologue and allows you to say something.<br>• If the person is creating a queue, try to give him or her something constructive to look at or do while you deal with the next person.<br>• Lean towards them when you want to speak and raise the palms of the hands outwards. |
| Superior | • Stay calm.<br>• Do not question his or her judgement or "throw" information at him or her.<br>• Flatter the knowledge he or she does possess but add to it with accurate information of your own.<br>• Use agreeing body language when you are supporting the information,<br>• Where possible, substantiate your knowledge with documentary evidence. |

**Techniques for handling difficult people continued**

| Type | Technique |
|------|-----------|
| Persistent questioner | <ul><li>Stay calm.</li><li>Be patient.</li><li>Repeat information as necessary.</li><li>Maintain an upright posture and use open palm gestures.</li><li>Provide reassurance.</li></ul> |
| Silent | <ul><li>Ask open questions which are relevant to the situation.</li><li>If there is no response immediately, do not force conversation on him or her but do indicate that you are available should help be needed.</li></ul> |

## *Some specific techniques*

There are some specific techniques which help in dealing with particular types of difficult people. Obviously the points made in the table above need to be adapted to suit individuals and should therefore be regarded as general guidelines.

The information in this chapter, combined with points from the preceding chapters, may be necessary if you become involved in resolving differences with other people and having to reach agreement — the subject of the next chapter.

# Chapter 7

## Negotiating Skills

You may be surprised to see a chapter on negotiating skills in a book for secretaries. You probably think of negotiating as belonging to the world of trade union officials and employers, and associated with wrangles over pay and conditions of work. In these circumstances it often seems to imply unpleasant conflict and the idea of one side winning and the other side losing.

In fact, negotiating is about resolving differences and about two or more people reaching agreement to their mutual satisfaction, a technique which is useful in a whole range of situations.

## Situations faced by secretaries which require negotiating skills

There are many occasions when secretaries need to use negotiating techniques. On some occasions this may be to obtain a concession from another person; on others it may be necessary to respond to a concession someone else wants. A range of such situations are shown below.

(a) Possible occasions when you may want others to make concessions:
- (i) Sharing an office with another secretary and wanting to change the office layout.
- (ii) Wanting further training from the company as part of career development.
- (iii) Wanting a discount on office equipment from a supplier.
- (iv) Requiring a refund on cancelled travel arrangements.
- (v) Wanting time off, a rise or changes in hours of work.
- (vi) Bargaining over price and facilities for a conference with a local hotel.

(b) Possible occasions when you are asked to make concessions:
- (i) A request to work late for several nights.
- (ii) A request to participate in training junior secretaries in the company.
- (iii) Another department wants to borrow some equipment.
- (iv) A client wants to arrange a meeting with the manager at a suitable location abroad.

---

### Action

It would be useful at this stage to list the situations at work when *you* may need negotiating skills.

---

Whatever the situation, when two people meet to arrange facilities, price, location, time, service, etc and have different ideas about what they want, it is possible for the encounter to go one of two ways:

(a) to reach an amicable agreement in which both parties feel they have achieved most of their objectives or

(b) to create bad relationships which have a long term harmful effect, because one party feels that it has not achieved its objectives.

It is therefore important to know the essentials of a good negotiation.

# The concept of a good negotiation

Negotiating well is an extension of assertiveness. It is standing up for one's own position but also allowing that the other person has rights too. Negotiations go wrong when people try to be too aggressive or are too submissive.

## *The problems of using dominance to resolve differences*

Have you ever won an argument by using some of the aggressive characteristics? You got your way but at what cost? When you use dominance to win, you turn the situation into a power struggle in which the other person has lost. When people lose, they feel angry and resentful and often try to get their own back on another occasion. Alternatively they feel annoyed with themselves, inadequate and humiliated. None of these reactions are very helpful in a work environment where you probably have to meet that person frequently or work with him or her daily.

## *The importance of mutual agreement*

Whenever you find yourself in a situation where you need to resolve differences with another person, you need to try to achieve what is known as a "win-win solution". The end result must be an agreement which meets the needs of both people so that each can feel satisfied with his or her own behaviour and so that good relationships are maintained.

You can achieve this if you follow some basic principles, go through the appropriate stages and use positive tactics.

# The basic principles

These principles apply to all negotiations:

(a) Aim for a win-win result which satisfies both sides.
(b) Always state your own position clearly and honestly; listen and respond to the other person so that you are both fully aware of the issues involved.
(c) Be prepared to make some concessions to achieve a result but do not let all the concessions be on your side — try to use "trade offs" (a concession from you for one in return).
(d) Try to make concessions which are cheap for you to make (in terms of money, time, effort, etc) but which will be valued highly by the other person.

(e) Do not rush into negotiations unprepared — give yourself, ask the other person for, time to prepare properly.

(f) Always check the final agreement.

# The five stages of a negotiation

There are five basic stages in any negotiation. These are:

(a) *prepare*
(b) *discuss*
(c) *signal movement*
(d) *propose*
(e) *agree.*

## *Prepare*

A successful result is largely dependent on good preparation. The majority of people cannot negotiate effectively "off the top of their heads". You need to prepare:

(a) the topics you want to talk about, i.e. the issues
(b) the ideal result you would like to achieve *and* also the realistic result you should expect
(c) the facts you will need to present
(d) the tactics you will need to use *and*
(e) anticipate what the other person is likely to put forward as his or her case.

## *Discuss*

When you meet the other person you need to:

(a) state your own position clearly and concisely in a calm, assertive manner
(b) listen attentively to the other person
(c) ask questions to clarify your understanding of his or her position (eg "am I right in thinking that you want . . .?")
(d) ask probing, open questions to secure more ideas and facts.

The discussion stage will:

(a) clarify the issues both sides want to raise
(b) show how close or far apart they are
(c) show where the concessions may be made.

## *Signal movement in your position*

A mere statement of two positions will not result in a productive agreement. At some stage, one person has to indicate that he or she might be willing to move (ie to make some kind of concession). This is probably the most difficult stage of the negotiation because both people feel that if they show any kind of movement in position it is a sign of weakness. You will therefore find that signals of movement are rather difficult to detect.

Some typical examples of signs of movement in another person are show below.

**Examples of signs of movement in a negotiation**

(a) *Listen for qualitative words* such as:
   (i)    maybe
   (ii)   perhaps
   (iii)  I might
   (iv)   well.
(b) *Look for body language signals* such as:
   (i)    leaning forward and looking keen
   (ii)   thoughtful evaluative gestures, eg rubbing chin
   (iii)  expectant facial expression, eg raised eyebrows and
          a pause in speech.

If the other person does not show these signs, then you can use them yourself.

(c) *Listen for or make tentative proposals*
   These are phrases such as:
   (i)    'If I were to . . ., would you be prepared to . . .?"
   (ii)   "I might be willing to . . ., however, I would expect
          you to . . ."

Such tentative proposals allow you to explore areas in which concessions and counter-concessions might be made but do not commit you until you know the other person's response.

## *Propose*

Once signals of movement have been exchanged, it is possible to make these tentative proposals on various issues and gradually firm them up. The possibilities contained in words such as "might", "could" or "would" become positive action in words such as "going to", "will" or "do".

## *Agree*

Once positive action has been agreed on all the issues, a settlement has been reached. The only stage now is to double check the full result so that both sides' interpretations of the agreement are the same. In some cases it may be necessary to confirm the agreement in a contract or by letter, etc.

These stages look simple to follow; of course it assumes that the other person is helpful and reasonable. At times you will encounter people who think that the main objective in any situation is to get their own way at any cost.

# Tactics used by aggressive negotiators

It is necessary to recognise the tactics used by such people and the reasons why they are using them. In all cases, the prime reason for such tactics is to make you lose control in some way so that they can turn this to their advantage and secure maximum concessions from you.

Once you understand their perception, it becomes easier to de-personalise the effects of their aggression and get on with a constructive negotiation.

| Tactic | Purpose |
|---|---|
| Being personally insulting. Making insinuations. Ridiculing your ideas. | To make you angry and lose control or to reduce you to a state of nerves; to make you lose control. |
| Accusing you of incompetence. | To undermine your confidence. |
| Accusing you of time wasting. | To force the pace of the negotiation so that you lose control. |
| Stating they cannot spend any more time. | To rush you into making inappropriate concessions. |
| Turning their back on you or walking away. | To rush you into making inappropriate concessions. |

Your response to any such tactics should be:

(a) to recognise them for what they are and avoid any emotional reaction
(b) to stay calm; control your speech and behaviour and use your assertiveness techniques
(c) in extreme cases, to withdraw from the negotiation and state you will return to the discussion as and when the other side is willing to listen.

## Positive negotiation tactics

There are several positive tactics you should employ to help achieve a positive result to any negotiation. These are:

(a) *listen actively* to the other person's points and then respond to each of these. Avoid the temptation to merely repeat your own points

(b) *ask probing questions* to check your understanding of the issues involved

(c) *show understanding, patience and interest* by words, tone and body language

(d) *speak clearly and confidently* using tactful language. Also control the speed of your speech and provide pauses to allow the other person to appreciate your points fully

(e) *use positive, assertive body language*

(f) *use round or oval tables* or sit side by side (this is seen as friendly and conversational).

Although the title of this chapter was negotiating skills, you may not use the word "negotiating" in many of the situations you encounter. You may think of each situation in terms of a problem to be resolved or ideas to be thrashed out in a discussion. However, whenever you are involved in differences in perception, attitudes, objectives or methods which are creating difficulties, negotiating skills combined with assertiveness techniques will play a useful role.

---

### Action

Now you have been introduced to the stages of a negotiating and the tactics you should use, try practising these techniques in a non-work situation first.

You could practise by reaching agreement:

(a) with a friend on a night out
(b) with a friend or spouse on your next holiday.

Perhaps there are more serious conflicts that need resolution by negotiating, eg:

(a) with a neighbour over some boundary or joint access dispute
(b) with a local garage or organisation over repairs or maintenance.

---

# Communicating in face to face encounters

| Do not | Do |
|---|---|
| • open your mouth without prior planning on how to achieve your purpose | • think carefully about the whole communication process |
| • allow the barriers to effective listening to distract you | • observe the basic rules for speaking and listening well |
| • allow words and body language to be contradictory | • use body language positively to reinforce a spoken message |
| • place too much emphasis on isolated body language signals from other people | • use clusters of body language signals to interpret other people's communication |
| • unwittingly upset others in your face to face encounters by ignoring basic courtesy | • consciously try to create a positive image of yourself and your company in *all* face to face encounters |
| • use aggressive or submissive behaviour in your encounters | • recognise situations which challenge your assertiveness and practise assertiveness techniques in such situations |
| • react emotionally to difficult people or label them as being "naturally" difficult | • recognise the possible reasons behind difficult behaviour and remain calmly professional in dealing with such people |
| • attempt to resolve differences using a win/lose attitude | • look for workable compromises to resolve differences |

## Communicating in face to face encounters continued

| Do not | Do |
|---|---|
| <ul><li>attempt to negotiate without good preparation</li><li>use the tactics of aggressive negotiators.</li></ul> | <ul><li>prepare well and go through all the appropriate stages of a good negotiation</li><li>use positive listening, speaking and body language tactics.</li></ul> |

# Section 3

## Communicating with Others (2)

### Objectives

By the end of this section you will be able to:

    (a) improve your own telephone techniques
    (b) take effective telephone messages
    (c) improve your style in written communication.

# Chapter 8

## Effective Telephone Communication

The telephone is the lifeline of most offices. Together with the fax machine, it is the most frequently used method of communicating inside and outside organisations. It is because the telephone is to hand and apparently simple to use that it can be so easily abused. As a secretary, you probably act as a "filter" for most of the calls to your manager as well as making many calls on his or her behalf. This chapter incorporates some ideas for making your telephone calls:

(a) less time consuming
(b) more cost-effective
(c) more assertive
(d) more successful.

However, it is useful to start with some of the complaints about telephone communication.

### Common telephone faults

Secretaries take numerous calls and are therefore in a good position to criticise other people's faults. The common complaints heard are:

(a) *Poor reception of a call*
- "So often the phone rings and rings — maybe for half a minute or more before someone answers it."

- "I get left hanging on by the switchboard without any indication that the extension's engaged. Alternatively, I get that awful electronic music and no-one bothers to let me know what is happening. It all wastes my time."

- "I get someone on the other end who thinks a 'Hello' is that that's necessary as a greeting. I waste my time trying to find out who I'm talking to."

- "There's nothing worse than someone who answers the phone by saying 'there's no-one here' when you're already talking to them!"

(b) *Poor attitude*
- "So many people who answer my phone calls sound bored, impatient or unpleasantly curt that I find it difficult to maintain a conversation with them."

- "Some people are very rude on the phone. They don't seem to want our business at all."

(c) *Poor listening*
- "I find some people are very poor listeners. Often it's the noise; I don't know what is going on at their end but it certainly affects their concentration."

- "Some people just don't seem to be able to listen. You constantly have to repeat things for them over and over again — it's so frustrating."

(d) *Poor organisation*
- "On countless occasions I have to wait while they go and find a pencil or a message pad; can't they have these items by the phone?"

- "I waste time hanging on the end of the phone while they pop off to look for the information in a file. They often say they won't be long but 'not long' can be five minutes sometimes."

(e) *Ineffective people*

- "There are some real wets in organisations. They can't do this or they can't find that — they sound so pathetic."

- "I would like to shake some of the people I have to talk to on the phone. They ramble on about this and that and never get to the point, let alone take the action I am wanting them to take."

This is quite a list of complaints and most people have had similar experiences.

---

**Action**

Look back over the quotes again. Are you absolutely sure that none of these criticisms can be levelled at you . . . ever?

---

# Use of other skills

If you are to avoid the criticisms above, all the skills mentioned in the previous section are also important in telephone communication, apart from body language.

You need:

(a) a knowledge of the basic communication process
(b) speaking skills
(c) listening skills
(d) assertiveness
(e) the ability to handle difficult people
(f) negotiating skills.

Instead of body language, you need to concentrate very heavily on your voice — its speed, its pitch and its tone. Having said this, it is a good idea to use appropriate body language when you are using the telephone — it can affect the way you sound!

# Your telephone voice

The voice is the main asset for creating the right image with other people. It can be used to catch their attention, to hold their attention, to elicit co-operation or to secure action. You need to pay attention to:

(a) what you say
(b) how you say it.

## *What you say*

The points you need to bear in mind are:

(a) *Use words to create a positive image of you*
Whether you are making or receiving calls, the other person
cannot see you in your office, observe how busy you are or know
what action you may be taking. You must therefore keep the
other person informed throughout the call.
(b) *Use words which the other person is likely to understand*
If the caller is a stranger, do not assume that he or she knows
the technical jargon of your company or of your department.
(c) *Do not use words which sound patronising or over-familiar*
Avoid calling people "luv" or "dear".
(d) There are *some words you need to use with care* because they can
convey the wrong "picture".

| *Word* | *Picture* |
| --- | --- |
| • "John is *busy* at present." It sounds like an excuse. | John is avoiding talking to you. |
| • "I would like to help *but* . . ." It sounds like a soft refusal — a negative response. | "I don't want to help at all." |
| • "I'm *terribly* sorry . . ." It may sound insincere. | "I'm not really sorry at all." |
| • 'I'll *try* to find him." The stressed word is not very reassuring. | "But I won't manage to locate him." |
| • "I *guarantee* it." Do not use the word "guarantee" unless fulfilment of the action is within your control. | Fingers crossed, it might happen. |
| • "I can't answer *that*." Claiming ignorance or reluctance to answer in one area of questioning may be ascribed to all other questions. | "I can't answer any of your questions." |

## *How you say it*

Your tone of voice conveys the way you are feeling about the other person and the conversation. Your tone can give away whether you are:

| | |
|---|---|
| ● negative | ● positive |
| ● bored | ● enthusiastic |
| ● aggressive | ● assertive |
| ● tired | ● alert |
| ● unsure | ● certain |
| ● rude | ● courteous |
| ● antagonistic | ● friendly |
| ● harassed | ● calm. |

However difficult the topic is to discuss and resolve, or however awkward the person on the other end of the phone appears to be, keep a positive tone in your voice.

Although the other person cannot see you, it is always a good idea to use positive body language:

(a) good posture and
(b) a smiling expression.

# Preparing for calls

Many faults can be overcome by good preparation, whether receiving or making calls.

## *Receiving calls*

You may think there is little preparation you can do for incoming calls since you cannot predict who will call and what they will want. However, there are some steps you can take to be prepared.

(a) *A good working knowledge of your organisation*
   This means knowing its products, services and people; the current project or tasks being undertaken by your manager; unconcluded business with clients, customers and business associates, etc.

(b) *A well-organised office and desk*

You can be ready for calls by having a pad and pencil to hand for taking down messages; the diary and appointments book to hand; the bring forward system, computer files or documentary files within easy reach of the desk, etc.

## Making calls

Your preparation for making calls can save you time and your organisation money.

(a) *Planning calls for the day*

Plan in advance, whenever possible, the calls you need to make that day.

(i)   Prioritise them in terms of importance and urgency to your manager or to you. Delay non-important, non-urgent calls until the cheaper rate times.

(ii)  Plan your time with the receiver in mind. There may be certain times of the day in the concerned business when he or she would not welcome phone calls or be receptive to your message. This is particularly important for international calls. You do not want to be ringing an overseas customer or client in the middle of the night.

(b) *Plan each call*

For each call:

(i)    decide in advance to whom you need to speak and check his or her number and extension. Decide whether there is anyone else who can help you if your contact is not available

(ii)   decide the purpose of the call. You need to have this clear in your mind in order to choose your vocabulary and tone

(iii)  make brief notes to cover all the points you want to make — tick them off as you achieve each one

(iv)   have any facts which may be needed in the course of the conversation to hand (ie the relevant file)

(v)    if you know it will be a difficult call, stand up to make the call — it helps you to remain assertive

(vi)   try to anticipate the problems associated with the call eg will the receiver be annoyed or resentful about the information. Think how you will use vocabulary, tone to deal with this.

# The verbal handshake

Any telephone conversation should start with a greeting and some preliminary information. This is known as the verbal handshake. Just as you would acknowledge a visitor's presence immediately, go up to him or her, extend your hand and introduce yourself; so you need to do the equivalent on the telephone. Also, adopt the slogan "Smile while you dial".

## Receiving calls

When answering the phone this means:

(a) *Answer promptly*
    Try to answer after the third or fourth ring.
(b) *Give a greeting*
    This should be:
    (i)    good morning or afternoon
    (ii)   your department
    (iii)  your name.
(c) *Offer assistance*
    Preferably this should be: "How can I help you?"
(d) *Sound friendly*
    Make the greeting in a tone of voice which sounds alert, enthusiastic and welcoming (even if you hate the interruption!).

## Making a call

When making a call observe the following rules.

(a) Respond to this initiation of the verbal handshake by announcing your name, your organisation and the purpose of your call.
(b) If your receiver makes no attempt to initiate the handshake, then you should give a full greeting. Again, remember to keep the greeting friendly even if the purpose of your call may be a complaint.
(c) If the receiver sounds cross, distracted or pre-occupied ask whether it is a convenient time to call. This gives him or her the opportunity to decide to take the call or offer to ring you back.

# Controlling the call

Whether you are a caller or a receiver, your telephone call is likely to involve giving, listening to or asking for information or summarising action.

## *Giving information*

Information should be given:

(a) *in a logical sequence*, so that the other person can follow your reasoning

(b) *in a clear voice with well-pronounced words*, so that the other person can hear and understand

(c) *at a slower speed* than your normal conversational pace, so that the other person has time to absorb the full impact of the message.

(d) *with a tone that reflects accurately the content of the message*, so that there is no contradiction between *what* is said and *how* it is said.

## *Listening to information*

All the rules of listening apply here. Some additional points are as follows:

(a) *Limit interruptions*
Allow the other person to deliver his or her full message; resist the temptation to interrupt or anticipate what he or she is going to say.

(b) *Demonstrate attention*
Pay particular attention to using "Mm", "I see", etc to demonstrate that you are still listening on the other end of the phone.

(c) *Concentrate on the call*
Do not attempt to carry on with word processing, sorting files, etc while listening just because the other person is unable to see you trying to do two things at once. If you have answered the phone, commit your full attention to the matter in hand.

(d) *Take notes*
During any phone call it should be an automatic response to note down key points: names, addresses, numbers, amounts, dates and times.

## *Asking for information*

In any exchange, it will be necessary to ask for information. There are two types of question to use:

(a) *Closed questions* — those which require a yes or no answer which should be reserved for checking the accuracy of information.

(b) *Open questions* — those starting with "which", "what", "when", "who", "why", "how", "where" when you want more details.

If you use these two types of question carefully and for the right purpose, you can limit the time of a call and avoid confusion or frustration.

## *Summarising action*

This is the way all calls should end. Once an exchange of information has taken place, both people need to be absolutely clear what the result of the conversation has been and what further action is to be taken.

Any summary should state clearly:

(a) what specific action will be taken
(b) by whom the action will be taken
(c) any deadline for the action to be taken.

Avoid vague phrases such as:

(a) "as soon as possible"
(b) "soon"
(c) "in the near future",

when referring to time. Precise times (ie "today", "tomorrow", "next Monday") are far more helpful.

# Confidentiality on the telephone

Apart from the basic telephone techniques mentioned above, it is also important to maintain privacy and confidentiality of information on the telephone.

(a) Ensure you have a system that allows you to talk privately to your manager in the middle of a call without the caller overhearing the conversation.

(b) Generally, be careful about what you say over the public telephone network. It is possible to get crossed lines and someone may overhear embarrassing information or be able to listen to confidential information.

(c) Customers, clients or competitors may attempt to "pump" you for confidential information. They often do this with great charm by asking a series of leading questions. If you are asked about:

(i)   the future plans of your manager or company
(ii)  company statistics
(iii) security procedures
(iv)  financial details
(v)   other employees' home addresses or telephone numbers

these are all likely to be items of confidential information. If you are unsure whether disclosure might be a breach of confidentiality or security you should take a note of the caller's name, telephone number, company and the exact information he or she wants and offer to ring back. You then have an opportunity to check the identity of the caller and the information required with your manager.

If you know that disclosure would be a breach of confidentiality, state politely that it is company policy not to disclose such information.

## Making calls to mobile telephones

Modern technology has created additional problems for telephone users — contacting people on mobile units. It is possible your own manager may have one of these or that he or she will ask you to ring a number you recognise as being one of the mobile systems.

Apart from all the telephone techniques already mentioned, it is useful to follow a few additional rules.

(a) *Anticipate the worst scenario for receiving the call*
    Obviously, it is not possible to see the circumstances in which

the receiver is taking the call, so anticipate the worst scenario (eg heavy traffic or an insecure location). Always check whether it is convenient for the receiver to take the call — offer him or her a chance to make a reasoned judgement about the safety or security of taking the call. After all, if he or she is taking the call while driving, that breaks the "not doing two things at once" rule.

(b) *Plan very carefully*

Be very precise in delivering the message so that the call is as short as possible. This limits the danger and keeps telephone costs down.

(c) *Give a telephone number*

Give your telephone number early in your message. It is possible to key telephone numbers into a mobile phone during a call and this allows the receiver the opportunity to ring you back if there is a break in the transmission or her or she meets hazardous conditions.

If you receive a call which you know is from a mobile telephone:

(a) *Give the call your full attention*

Then the other person does not have to repeat information.

(b) *Keep strictly to the purpose of the call*

Do not indulge in unnecessary conversation.

(c) *Avoid reacting to negative tone*

Do not react adversely if the other person's tone is anxious, curt, abrupt or impatient — it is probably due to the environment in which the call is being made.

While telephone contact is easy and convenient for dealing with many business matters, there are occasions when the written word is necessary. This is dealt with in the next chapter.

to compose routine letters and memos than spend time before them

# Chapter 9

## Improving Written Communication

Most secretarial courses teach the rudiments of letter, memo and report layout as part of their programme and most secretaries have probably been told by managers or training officers at induction about the format preferred by their own organisations. Therefore, no purpose will be served by going over the basics here. Instead, this chapter concentrates on aspects which may improve the style of written communication.

## Importance of writing skills

Earlier chapters have stated how good personal secretaries should be able to relieve managers of some of the administrative aspects of their jobs; the planning and composition of letters, memos and reports can be part of this work. For example, if you are researching information, then it is logical to present the results to your manager in an information report. If you are handling the post, then it is often easier for you to compose routine letters and memos than spend time having them dictated by your manager.

These are elements of your secretarial role that you may need to discuss with your manager and you may need to prove to him or her that you can be relied upon to produce accurate documents that are appropriate to the situation in terms of content and style.

# Improving a manager's written communication

It is a critical time when a secretary takes over the composition of some written documents from a manager. It is far too easy to be critical of the manager's style of writing and to change the style completely when responsibility is delegated. A tactful secretary will make gradual changes and be open to discussion about the use of particular phrases or tone — remember assertiveness techniques!

For example, you may decide that your manager's demand for immediate payment of an invoice is too brusque to be sent to a customer after only seven days have elapsed. You could introduce your changes by saying to your manager:

> "I thought I'd express our request for payment in this way because it accepts the possibility that our letter and their cheque may have crossed in the post. Do you agree?".

A good secretary, by gradual, tactful handling, can subtly change the manager's attitude towards written correspondence from poor practice into a good writing style. Do not expect an immediate recognition of your abilities and open appreciation of your suggestions — most of us are reluctant to admit our own failings freely to others. What you may notice is a gradual adoption of some of your own phrases and ideas into his or her own composition.

The rest of this chapter will be devoted to some of the finer points about written communication, pointing out some common faults in writing and how to avoid them.

# When to write

The first important decision to make is whether to communicate in writing or orally. There are some guidelines to bear in mind.

(a) Facts are better conveyed in writing; feelings and opinions are better expressed face to face.

(b) Written communication is often needed to follow up oral communication when:

(i)    the correct information needs to be confirmed

(ii)   the information needs to be on record for future reference

(iii)  the same detailed information needs to be conveyed to a number of people at the same time.

(c) It is not possible to control the place or feelings of the person receiving written communication and therefore the content and style must be exactly right for the situation to induce the right response.

(d) Feedback from written communication is slower to arrive than that from oral communication.

It is important to choose the most appropriate method, or combination of methods, of communication, to achieve the intended purpose. Using the wrong method is just one of the mistakes that can be made. The next section will deal with some others.

## Common faults in written communication

There are some very common faults to which most writers fall prey and it is useful to be able to identify these in one's own writing and that of others. The table on page 108 will identify the main faults and why they are considered to be inappropriate.

All these faults are likely to alienate the reader and either delay the reply or induce an inappropriate response. The next few sections will look at ways of remedying these faults.

## Keeping writing short and simple

The aim of business writing is to enable the reader to understand the message quickly and easily. This can be remembered easily in the mnemonic KISS:

**K**   keep

**I**    it

**S**   short and

**S**   simple.

## The nature of common writing faults

| Fault | Result |
|---|---|
| Writing is too long-winded, eg:<br><br>● long rambling reports<br>● letters using long paragraphs and sentences<br>● memos running to a continuation sheet. | The reader puts off reading the document for as long as possible.<br><br>The reader has to read through the material more than once to make sense of the contents. |
| Writing is too obscure, eg:<br><br>● complicated words<br>● ambiguous<br>● inappropriate words<br>● complex sentences<br>● inappropriate sequence of information. | The reader has to read the material several times to make sense of the contents.<br><br>The meaning of the correspondence may not be clear and the reader will have to ask for clarification.<br><br>The reader may think you are deliberately trying to confuse him or her or being officious. |
| Writing uses the wrong tone eg:<br><br>● too curt<br>● too patronising<br>● too familiar. | The reader is annoyed or resentful and feels unco-operative.<br><br>The reader does not want to respond. |
| Writing is full of use of English faults, eg:<br><br>● poor spelling<br>● poor punctuation<br>● poor sentence construction. | The reader receives a poor impression of the writer and the organisation<br><br>If use of English is inaccurate the reader may doubt the accuracy of the content. |

Any business document should only be the length needed to include all the relevant facts. The purpose of business writing is to provide information for, and invoke a response from, the reader, — not to display the literary talent of the writer. In practice this means:

(a) making correct use of paragraphing
(b) keeping sentence construction simple but varying the length of sentences
(c) eliminating unnecessary adjectives and adverbs from sentences.

## *Paragraphing*

The most common faults in paragraphing are:

(a) not using paragraphs at all
(b) using a new paragraph for each sentence
(c) grouping random points within a paragraph.

The basic principle for paragraphing is that each new aspect of a topic needs a new paragraph. Once the aspect to be covered in a paragraph has been decided, related points need to be grouped together within the paragraph.

For example, a letter making a simple complaint may have four paragraphs. The aspect to be covered in each paragraph is as follows:

### Example of paragraphing in a letter of complaint

| | |
|---|---|
| *Paragraph 1* – | introduces the reader to the nature of the complaint and the context in which the complaint is being made. |
| *Paragraph 2* – | provides details of the nature of the complaint. |
| *Paragraph 3* – | explains the implications for the writer such as loss of business, time, inconvenience, etc. |
| *Paragraph 4* – | states what action the complainant wants taken to remedy the situation. |

An example of such a letter appears on page 110.

## Example of letter making a complaint

| Wells | High Class Butchers |
| :--- | :--- |
| **&** | 10 The Withies, OCKINGHAM, |
| **Gough** | Beckhampshire OF6 1XP |
| | Telephone: 0666 57890 |

5 September 19 . .

The Manager
Royal Hotel
Western Parade
OCKINGHAM
Beckhampshire OK3 2RG

Dear Sir

**Duty telephonist 1 September 19 . .**

On 1 September 19 . ., I telephoned your hotel to tell your Assistant Catering Manager, John Bowman, about problems in securing game birds for the celebration dinner that evening. I found the duty telephonist that day rude and unhelpful.

The facts are as follows. I attempted to make contact three times. The first time she assumed I was asking for a guest and put the phone down before I had time to correct her. When I redialled, she accused me of not knowing what I wanted and wasting her time. She then left me waiting to be put through for five minutes. When I tried later that morning, I was told curtly that Mr Bowman was out and there was no-one else who could take my call. Since the matter had become urgent, I had to visit the hotel personally to resolve it. I found that Mr Bowman had been in the hotel all morning.

This encounter made me feel annoyed, put me to unnecessary trouble and did very little for the reputation of your hotel. Since other clients and suppliers may be receiving similar treatment, I decided to make a formal written complaint.

I hope you will be able to improve your telephonist's behaviour and would appreciate reassurance that corrective action has been taken.

Yours faithfully

M Gough

## *Sentence construction*

Many people believe that long, complicated sentences demonstrate a good command of the English language. This is not always the case in business correspondence. When a writer uses long, complicated sentences it is more difficult to detect the main ideas and there is more chance that the sentence will contain syntax errors.

### Example of a long, complicated sentence

Read the following sentence. Can you make sense of it on the first reading?

Since long complex sentences lend themselves to obscurity and are incomprehensible to many it is probably best to avoid them as most writers consistently advise, bearing in mind, of course, that it may be impossible to break some sentences down, although this is rare, since most sentences consist of numerous subordinate clauses which can usually be divided into separate sentences if you wish to observe the principle that one idea per sentence is sufficient for a reader to digest at any given time.

Although this sentence contains useful information, it is difficult for the reader to extract it because of the complicated sentence construction.

The principles of good sentence construction for business writing are:

(a) use simple sentences
(b) each sentence should contain a single idea.

This does not mean that every sentence has to be very short; this would give the writing a disjointed, staccato style. Varying the length of sentences provides a good flowing style.

See how much easier it is to understand the content of the example passage when divided into the following sentences.

Most writers advise that, as long complex sentences lend themselves to obscurity and are incomprehensible to many, it is better to avoid them. Of course, it may be impossible to break down some sentences. However, this is rare, since most sentences consist of numerous subordinate clauses, which can usually be divided up into separate sentences. This observes the principle that one idea per sentence is sufficient for a reader to digest at any given time.

If you keep to shorter, simpler sentences, your sentence construction is likely to be correct.

## *Use of adjectives and adverbs*

Some writers embellish their letters and memos with frequent use of adjectives and adverbs. For examples

It is a matter of the *utmost* urgency.
This offer is *totally* unique.
You are assured of my *very best* attention.

In most business correspondence and in reports, the frequent use of adjectives and adverbs is inappropriate. It is the facts which need to be conveyed; adjectives and adverbs often carry emotional overtones and can contribute to an impression of effusiveness, patronisation or insincerity.

The exception to this basic principle is in promotional letters or those attempting to persuade. The contrast between the two approaches can be seen in the letters on pages 113 and 114.

# Keeping writing clear and direct

The points made in the previous section will contribute to clear and direct writing. Some other aspects to bear in mind are:

(a) choosing appropriate words and phrases
(b) eliminating "officialese"
(c) developing an appropriate sequence for presenting information.

## *Choosing appropriate words and phrases*

We can all make our writing more complicated than necessary by using complex or incorrect words and unnecessary phrases.

### *Use simple direct words*

Always try to use the simplest, most direct word to suit the situation. Again, there is no place in business correspondence for trying to impress readers with one's command of three or four syllable words. Simpler words are recognised more quickly and help understanding.

**Example of factual letter**

## *National Leisure Ltd*

# 31-33 Oxford Square, London W.1

Telephone: 071-666 2489 Fax: 071-666 2597

5 September 19. .

Mr A Cook
Country Craft Kitchens Ltd
10 The Links
OCKINGHAM
Beckhampshire OK5 6PL

Dear Mr Cook

**Your quotation 1207 for design and installation of kitchen fittings**

I am pleased to tell you that National Leisure Ltd have accepted your quotation for the design and installation of kitchen fittings for our new teashop at the Waterloo Country Park in Ockingham.

You will be receiving an official order for this work within the next three days. We will need the installation to be completed by 5 April 19. . , so that the teashop can open for business at the beginning of the Easter holiday.

I would like to meet you early next week to discuss the plans you submitted. I suggest Tuesday 13 September at 11.00 am in the reception area of the Waterloo Country Park. Could you confirm the date and time with me by telephone on the above number, extension 35?

Yours sincerely

P Fox
Development Manager

## Example of a promotional letter

(NB This would be produced by mailmerge so space has been left for the personalised details, eg name of contact, name of organisation, etc.)

# Stinton Training

19 Russley Green Wokingham
Berks WK6 5PP
Telephone: 0739 71794

5 November 19. .

Dear (space for personalised name)

**Can you meet the challenge of the 1990s?**

The 1990s will be a period of rapid change in which only organisations with a well-trained workforce will survive. Does (space for inserting company name) want to meet this challenge? If so, WE can help you.

Our organisation has over fifteen years' experience in training staff from top British companies. The courses we offer can be tailor-made to the special needs of (space for inserting company names) and can take place on (space for company name) premises or at suitable hotel complexes — the choice is yours!

Our trainers are experienced in a wide range of management skills including: total quality and customer care, team building, negotiation, managing change. Perhaps your staff need a "crash" course in foreign languages to handle delicate overseas contracts. We can make them proficient in French, German or Spanish in three weeks; Japanese and Russian take a little longer.

If you have a training need, STINTON TRAINING can help YOU. Don't be left behind! Send for our FREE BROCHURE today, or contact Sue on the above number. The rest is up to us!

Yours sincerely

B Kempworthy
Director

## *Simple vocabulary*

Do not use complex language in written communication. It is important that the reader understands the message — preferably on the first reading. Imagine the effect of complex language on someone to whom you are speaking — they frown or look blank and say "pardon" or "could you repeat that?" The reader's reaction is likely to be the same if the language is too complex.

For example:

| *avoid* | *use* |
|---------|-------|
| ● commencement | ● start |
| ● optimum | ● best |
| ● utilise | ● use |

This does not mean that all long words have to be avoided; merely note that if you use too many together it makes your writing more obscure — it "fogs" the reader.

---

## Action

*Checking the fog factor*
There is a simple way to check whether your sentences and use of vocabulary are simple and direct. It is called "checking the fog factor".

1. Take a page of writing (the content of a letter or memo, or the page of a report).
2. Count the number of words of three syllables or more on that page (eg sy-lla-bles).
3. Count the number of sentences on that page.
4. Divide the number of sentences into the number of words,

ie $\dfrac{\text{Number of words of three syllables or more}}{\text{Number of sentences}} = \text{fog factor}$

The principle is that the lower the fog factor number the easier it is to understand the information.
Try this calculation on your own writing.

## *Use precise words*

Always choose words with care. Use the exact word to suit the situation rather than a vague word or phrase which has many interpretations. Some vague words and phrases to avoid are:

- nice
- things
- and so on.

Avoid using technical terms (jargon) or abbreviations if there is any chance that these may not be understood by the reader.

## *Use the correct word*

There are several words in English that look and sound the same or similar but which have different meanings. It is important to use the right word. Some that may cause difficulty are shown below.

### **Similar words but different meanings**

| | |
|---|---|
| • affect<br>effect | • alternately<br>alternatively |
| • complement<br>compliment | • continual<br>continuous |
| • council<br>counsel | • dependant<br>dependent |
| • discreet<br>discrete | • principal<br>principle |

## *Eliminate unnecessary phrases*

Many people use a writing style which includes the use of words or phrases which are unnecessary since they add nothing to the message. Some examples of these are:

- "I am writing . . ."(They already know that.)
- "May I take this opportunity to say . . ."(You are going to, anyway!)
- "No doubt you are aware of the fact that . . ."(If they are aware, why say so.)
- "I, personally, . . ."(It must be you.)

## *Eliminate "officialese"*

"Officialese" means out-dated phrases which used to appear in Government correspondence but which are now considered stilted and inappropriate because the meaning can be expressed more directly. Some examples are shown below.

| *Avoid* | *Replace by* |
|---|---|
| ● We are in receipt of your esteemed communication of . . . | We have received your letter dated . . . |
| ● Please do not hesitate to . . . | Please . . . |
| ● in the not too distant future | soon |
| ● at an early date | soon |
| ● at the present moment in time | now |
| ● due to the fact that . . . | because |
| ● in consequence of . . . | because |
| ● a large proportion/number | many |
| ● a small proportion/number | a few |
| ● in view of the fact that | since |
| ● despite the fact that | although |
| ● draw your attention to the fact that | point out |
| ● give consideration to | consider |
| ● of the opinion that | think |

## *Use an appropriate sequence for the information*

Any business communication should be written for the ease of the reader, not that of the writer. This means choosing a sequence for presenting the information that will be logical for the reader to follow. This is true of report writing as well as letter and memo writing.

### *Report writing*

There are conventions about the sections for reports; you may have covered this in a secretarial course.

## Sequence for an information report

If the report is presenting a summary of existing information (information report) it is usual to present the information under:

(a) *Introduction:* this identifies what the report is about and why it is needed.
(b) *Main body:* this section is organised under appropriate side headings and sub-headings and presents the facts in a logical sequence.
(c) *Conclusion:* This section draws the reader's attention to the main points.

An example of an information report is shown on page 119.

## Sequence for an investigation report

This type of report shows the methods used to investigate a particular situation or problem, what findings result from the investigation, draws conclusions and may then present proposals for future action. The sections which show this logical sequence are:

(a) *Terms of reference/Introduction:* this identifies what the report is about, why it is needed and any relevant background information.
(b) *Methods of investigation:* this explains the methods used to carry out the investigation (surveys, interviews, observation; use of books, articles, company records or statistics).
(c) *Findings/Analysis of information:* this section records the facts resulting from the investigation. Again in this type of report information will be organised under appropriate sub-headings.
(d) *Conclusions:* this presents the conclusions which can be drawn from the previous section's facts.
(e) *Recommendations:* this presents proposals for future action based on the facts already recorded.

An example of an investigation report is shown on page 121.

**Example of an information report**

REPORT ON ONE-DAY TRAINING COURSE FOR LEGAL
SECRETARIES ON CLIENT RELATIONS

1.  INTRODUCTION

Two secretaries from the Ockingham practice of Rushmoor,
Rushmoor & Field attended the above course at the Royal
Hotel  on Tuesday 12 March 19. . . They were asked to compile
a report on this and to submit it to the Practice Manager by 18
March 19. .. The purpose of the report was to provide
information concerning the course for all secretarial and
clerical staff in the various practice offices.

2.  ANALYSIS FOR INFORMATION

2.1   Content

The course was divided into three sessions:

2.1.1    Client relations conducted by letter: 2 hours.
2.1.2    Client relations conducted by telephone: 3 hours.
2.1.3    Face to face encounters with clients: 3 hours.

2.2   Training methods

2.2.1    Letters to clients
         –  The layout and style of letters required by
            solicitors was discussed by the trainer and
            a guidance hand-out was supplied.
         –  Examples of clients' letters to solicitors
            which requested information, guidance or
            complained about poor service were studied
            by course members in pairs and answers
            were prepared.
         –  These were then compared within the group
            with reference to layout, style, approach and
            diplomacy, and some general principles were
            drawn up on the flip-chart.

2.2.2   Telephone communication with clients
- A training video was shown which demonstrated the right and wrong ways of behaving on the telephone.
- Trainees were then divided into pairs and given roles, one as a client one as a secretary. Practice calls were then carried out, recorded and played back to the whole group. These were discussed and some general principles recorded.

2.2.3   Face to face encounters with clients
- A lecture was given by the trainer on the major problems and how to deal with them.
- A video was shown illustrating methods of dealing with typical client problems.
- The trainees were again divided into pairs and given roles; the encounters were filmed, played back to the whole group and discussed. Some general principles were recorded.

## 3. CONCLUSIONS

The secretaries who attended from this practice agreed that the course was worthwhile; it gave useful practice in handling situations which they have to face. This was very valuable as a preparation for communicating with clients diplomatically. It was also interesting to share experience and knowledge with trainees from other legal practices.


Signed................................................................


..........................................................


Date

**Example of investigation report (short)**

THE FEASIBILITY OF INTRODUCING FLEXI-TIME TO
THE CLERICAL AND ADMINISTRATIVE STAFF AT
WORTHINGTONS PLC

1   TERMS OF REFERENCE

The Personnel Director requested the Personnel Manager of the
Lancashire plant to investigate the possibilities of introducing
flexi-time to the staff within the General office.
A report was to be forwarded not later than 10 May 19. . so that it
could be discussed at the Personnel Managers' meeting at Head
Office.

2.   METHODS OF INVESTIGATION

The following methods were used.

2.1   A range of published material on flexi-time was read
including published articles concerning similar
organisations and equivalent members of staff.

2.2   A cross-section of staff within the General office was
interviewed to find out their views.

2.3   The Information Services Manager at Lows Ltd and the
Management Services Manager at Marchants plc were
visited to see their flexi-time system in operation.

3.   ANALYSIS OF INFORMATION

3.1   Advantage for management

The following advantages were noted:

    —   Less time was taken off by staff for essential
appointments.

    —   There was greater motivation amongst the staff
leading to higher productivity.

These advantages were found in both companies already
operating flexi-time.

3.2 Disadvantages for management

There was an initial difficulty in establishing a suitable core time and some early problems in controlling work flow. These were usually overcome within the first few weeks of the system being introduced.

3.3 Advantages for staff

All the staff interviewed mentioned that:

— they would be able to organise domestic arrangements more freely which would lead to less stress;

— they would have freedom to control when they arrived and departed and this would help with transport and punctuality;

— they would enjoy the sense of trust and responsibility.

3.4 Disadvantages for staff

Some staff expressed concern that liaison both within the department and with other departments might be more difficult. They stipulated that a clear and adequate core time must be established.

4. CONCLUSIONS

4.1 The advantages for both staff and management appear to outweigh the disadvantages; motivation and productivity would both be increased.

4.2 There is a need to establish sufficient core time and to develop clear procedures for control and liaison.

5. RECOMMENDATIONS

The following recommendations are made:

5.1 Flexi-time should be introduced within the General Office and given a trial period of three months.

5.2 Consultation should now take place between the Personnel Manager and the Office Supervisor about the most appropriate core time and control/liaison procedures.

5.3   The system introduced should be subject to careful briefing and close monitoring during the three month period.

5.4   The final decision concerning whether to retain the system and, if so whether to make any modifications, should be made at the end of the three month trial period.

Signed:

Dated:

In long reports (either information or investigation) it would be appropriate to present the reader with a brief summary of the conclusions and recommendations at the beginning of the report. This allows them to extract the most important facts quickly.

When supportive illustrations or data need to be included in a report which might distract the reader if included in the main body, it is customary to put such data in appendices at the end of the report but refer to the appendix in the main text eg (see Appendix . . .).

## *Letter writing*

Again, the main principle is to present information in an order which is appropriate for the reader. Generally the sequence is:

(a) opening paragraph — used to put the message into context
(b) middle paragraph(s) — develop the details of the message. In complex letters several middle paragraphs may be needed, each dealing with a different aspect of the message
(c) closing paragraph — states the action which is needed from the reader.

All letters conveying neutral information can follow this basic structure (ie letters of enquiry and reply).

*Letters conveying good news,* such as congratulations or those announcing the award of a contract, will follow the basic structure. However, it is important to state the good news clearly in the first paragraph of the letter.

*Letters giving bad news* need greater tact so as not to upset or offend the reader. Too often the bad news is baldly stated in the opening paragraph or added on (almost as an afterthought) in the closing paragraph. When conveying bad news it is necessary to prepare the reader in the earlier parts of the letter. In these circumstances the sequence to use is:

(a) *opening paragraph* — is used to explain the context and circumstances surrounding the bad news so that the reader is mentally prepared
(b) *middle paragraph* — explain further events or circumstances, state the bad news clearly but add any compensating factors or any statements which seek to alleviate any negative feelings likely to be experienced by the reader
(c) *closing paragraph* — states any future action which should or could be taken by the reader.

A copy of a letter following this sequence can be found on page 125.

# Maintaining the right tone

This may be one of the most difficult aspects of written communication, particularly in letters and memos. The tone of any piece of writing is apparent from the choice of words, phrases, types of noun and verb, and the use of any adjectives, adverbs and personal pronouns.

The main points to bear in mind when determining the right tone for a written communication are:

(a) to make the tone consistent with the purpose of the piece of writing
(b) to think about the characteristics of the readers and what will induce the best response from them.

## *Report writing*

The main purpose of a report is to present factual information clearly and concisely so that readers can make decisions based on facts.

Since it is the facts that are important, not the personal feelings or opinions of the writer, report writing should be formal and impersonal.

# Example of a letter conveying bad news

**Save & Build Building Society**
62 High Street,
Deddingham,
Dedhamshire DG6 2XO
Tel: 0963-72843
Fax: 0963-74382

5 September 19. .

Mr S March
The Willows
Cross Street
DEDDINGHAM
Dedhamshire DE1 5SN

Dear Mr March

**Mortgage application**

The Society has now completed its investigations and survey on Stable Cottage, Minkles Lane, Deddingham and I enclose a copy of the surveyor's report.

The surveyor found a number of faults, the most serious of which are:

- evidence of subsidence in part of the house;
- weak roofing supports;
- signs of wet rot in most timber frames.

Generally, the house is in a very poor state of repair. The Society has therefore decided that it cannot make you a mortgage offer on this property.

However, I must emphasise that the decision applies only to Stable Cottage. Save & Build Building Society would be happy to consider any mortgage application from you on another property. Please telephone me on the above number if you have any queries concerning the surveyor's report.

Yours sincerely

D Catherall
Mortgage Applications Manager

Enc: Surveyor's report

125

This means:

(a) use of concrete rather than abstract nouns
(b) sparing use of adjectives and adverbs
(c) avoidance of the personal pronouns "I" or "we", particularly when linked to emotive or personal preference or opinion (such as "I feel", "I prefer", "in my opinion", "I think").

This helps to maintain objectivity and allows the reader to see that the conclusions and recommendations are based on fact rather than personal ideas.

## Letters and memos

These are a little more difficult than reports. This is because organisations have their own "house style" for letters and managers have their own preferences, apart from the basic consideration of purpose and reader.

For example, the house style of an organisation may indicate that the use of the first person plural "we" in letters to indicate that it is the organisation rather than the individual who is conducting business. If no such rule exists, your manager may prefer you to write letters on his or her behalf and refer to him or her by name, eg "Mr Jones would like you to meet him . . .". Obviously you must observe any rules laid down by your organisation or your manager.

(a) *Neutral letters*

These are factual and use concrete nouns, make limited use of adjectives and adverbs and have a relatively impersonal style. As in the report, it is the facts which are important. The impersonality can be softened a little by using the active rather than the passive voice for the verb:

Not "An investigation will be carried out into . . ."
but "We shall investigate . . .".

(b) *Good news letters*

These are likely to use a mixture of concrete and abstract nouns, more emotive verbs and a more friendly style. The use of the personal pronoun "I" or "we" and the active voice of the noun is important in these letters eg:

not "Our congratulations are offered to you . . ."
but "We congratulate you on . . .".

(c) *Bad news letters*

These need to use a clear vocabulary with concrete nouns but some use of abstract nouns such as "understand", "appreciate", and of words such as "although" and "nevertheless" may be appropriate to cushion the bad news.

For example:

"Although we have refused your request to attend the training course on . . ., we do appreciate the importance of staff development. We therefore suggest that . . ."

(d) *Promotional / selling letters*

These will use abstract nouns as well as adjectives and adverbs more freely. They also employ rhetorical questions to get the readers to consider their need for the product or service, eg:

"Can you afford to ignore this amazing offer?".

They will also draw upon well known cliches or slang terms to deliver their message (to be avoided in other types of letter).

## *Characteristics of the reader and tone*

### *Circular letters and memos*

A standard circular letter which will go to several customers, clients or suppliers should be composed of words and phrases which will be understood by all of them and will not offend any of them. It is necessary to consider a "stereotype" to represent all the recipients and write for that type of person.

### *Letters and memos to individuals*

When you are writing to an individual, you need to use all your knowledge about that person. You may be able to derive this from personal knowledge or by reading any past correspondence from him or her. Writing needs to be adapted to the individual's:

(a) knowledge of the subject
(b) level of authority
(c) degree of familiarity with you in terms of a business relationship
(d) age.

If you lack knowledge about the reader, then you should maintain a relatively formal tone until your have more information on which to base your approach.

Choosing the right tone may be particularly difficult when writing internal memos. Despite a friendly open manner in face to face contact, some managers like their authority to be reinforced by receiving memos addressed to them in a formal, impersonal tone.

## Example of a memo using a formal tone

| | |
|---|---|
| TO: F Jones<br>Chief Accountant | FROM: E Miles<br>Secretary to Managing Director |
| DATE: 18 February 199. | SUBJECT: End of year accounts |

I am confirming the Managing Director's meeting with you for 20 February at 10.00 a.m. in his office.

Others welcome a friendly, informal approach.

## Example of a memo using a more informal tone

| | |
|---|---|
| TO: F Jones<br>Chief Accountant | FROM: E Miles<br>Secretary to Managing Director |
| DATE: 18 February 199. | SUBJECT: End of year accounts |

John says 10.00 a.m. in his office is OK for Tuesday.

Again, a good rule to follow is to maintain a rather formal tone with those who are on a superior level of authority within the organisation until you know their preferences. You can usually adopt a more relaxed informal style with those who are your equals or with subordinates.

However, even here you need to be careful since the purpose of the communication is relevant. The tone of a memo should not contradict the contents. For example, it is possible to trivialise an important instruction or idea by adopting an "over-chatty" tone. On the other hand, some of the pleasure of a memo congratulating a colleague is removed by a stiff and formal style.

# Writing press releases

This is a different form of writing, although the basic principles still remain true (ie straightforward vocabulary, simple direct sentences). Again, the important criterion is to put yourself in the place of the readers of the newspaper article in terms of deciding:

(a) all the facts that they will want to know
(b) the style of presentation that will make them attend to the article.

In addition, remember that:

(a) the heading and the first sentence are extremely important as they must attract the editor to stop and look at the rest of the passage
(b) facts and figures must be worked into a vivid description to make the article interesting to the reader
(c) editors are concerned with a fresh outlook, or a "human interest angle" on the facts.

In terms of layout, bear the following points in mind.

(a) Type the press release on the organisation's headed paper; this provides essential information.
(b) Give a contact name and extension number at the top of the page so that the editor can raise any queries with the right person.
(c) Mark the sheet "Press Release" so that it can be recognised quickly and easily.
(d) Indicate at the top whether it for "immediate release" or "to be released after ___ " (insert date).
(e) Use double line spacing and wide margins on either side of the paper so that there is room for editorial comment.
(f) Date the press release.

Finally, have the draft checked thoroughly before it is sent out to ensure that the facts are accurate and that no confidential information has been released.

# Producing accurate written communication

Although there is a saying "You should not judge a book by its cover" we are all tempted to assess the contents of published material or any piece of writing by its overall appearance. This will apply to your own writing. If a letter:

(a) looks disorganised because of poor layout
(b) is addressed incorrectly
(c) has incorrect used of English, including spelling, punctuation and sentence construction,

the reader is likely to be dubious about the accuracy of its content.

## *Good layout*

Make sure that every report, letter, memo, press release or set of minutes looks attractive. This means paying attention to the overall appearance of the words on the page. Apart from the conventions of various layouts which you probably know already, it means paying special attention to:

(a) using appropriate and prominent subject headings
(b) giving references where appropriate
(c) making good use of blank space around the text to make the layout look attractive
(d) making sure the print is easy to read.

## *Properly addressed*

Ensure that you do everything possible to enable your communication to reach its destination quickly.

(a) Check the name, sex, title and position of the person to whom the document is addressed. If you provide the full name and position of the recipient it should help the post room at the receiving organisation. Also, many recipients can be irritated by an incorrect initial or wrong form of title (ie Mr to a female).
(b) Ensure the full address with postcode is given.

## *Correct use of English*

If you provide a letter which has the correct use of English it is likely to indicate to your reader that you bother to proof-read your material and therefore that you have probably checked the accuracy of the content as well.

Poor use of English can indicate a careless "take it or leave it" attitude to communication in general.

---

**Action**

The best way to improve your use of English is to obtain a short, simple guide such as *Get it right* by Michael Temple (John Murray) and check any time you are uncertain.

---

# Check lists for written communication

This section provides some useful check lists for different forms of written communication.

## *Letters/memos*

Before writing a letter or memo:

    (a) Check the purpose of the letter or memo and consider what you know about the reader.
    (b) Collect or select accurate information only for inclusion.
    (c) Consider the appropriate tone to achieve the right response from the reader.
    (d) Apply the expected house style.

Points to consider after writing the letter or memo:

    (a) Does the overall appearance of the letter create a good impression of the writer and the organisation?
    (b) Have the conventions of letter or memo layout been followed?
    (c) Is the purpose of the letter or memo clear?
    (d) Does the letter or memo convey the correct information in sufficient detail to achieve its purpose?
    (e) Has the information been presented in the most logical sequence for the reader?

(f) Has paragraphing been used properly?

(g) Is the language and sentence construction simple, direct and appropriate for the reader?

(h) Is the tone appropriate for the purpose and the reader?

(i) Are spelling, punctuation and use of English correct?

(j) Is the overall message, however unpleasant, presented in a courteous manner?

## *Reports*

Before writing a report ask yourself the following questions:

(a) Are you clear about the purpose of the report, its scope and who will be reading it?

(b) Have you identified the appropriate sources of information (information report) or methods of investigation (investigation report)?

(c) Have you established some criteria for selecting the information to go into the report and for discarding trivia or irrelevancies?

(d) Does your organisation have a house style for writing reports?

After writing the report:

(a) Does the report have a title page or a heading which clearly indicates the subject?

(b) Is it clear to whom the report is addressed, who has compiled it and when it was written?

(c) Does the report have the appropriate sections depending on whether it is an information or investigation report?

(d) Have the facts been presented as concisely as possible?

(e) Have related points been grouped together under appropriate side headings and sub-headings?

(f) Is the sequence in which information is presented logical for the reader(s) to follow?

(g) Are the conclusions drawn directly from the facts presented in the main body of the report?

(h) Are the proposed recommendations based entirely on the facts presented in the main body of the report and in the conclusions?

(i) Has each section, side heading and sub-heading a numerical or alpha/numerical reference?

(j) Is the style of the report impersonal and formal?

(k) Are there any spelling, punctuation or use of English faults?

(l) Has the report been signed and dated at the end?

## Communicating with others (2)

| Do not | Do |
|---|---|
| ● allow any of the common telephone faults to be typical of your telephone technique. | ● ensure you plan your calls and use positive telephone techniques. |
| ● allow your words or your tone on the telephone to convey the wrong message. | ● adopt an appropriate telephone voice. |
| ● use vague greetings on the telephone. | ● use the verbal handshake. |
| ● waste your own and other people's time by poor organisation and control of calls. | ● control calls effectively. |
| ● allow yourself to be "pumped" for confidential information. | ● maintain confidentiality. |
| ● assume writing style is unimportant. | ● recognise the contribution of good written communication to successful business. |
| ● openly criticise other people's writing styles. | ● work tactfully to help other people improve their writing style. |
| ● lapse into any of the common writing faults. | ● keep your writing short and simple, clear and direct, and always keep your purpose and the reader uppermost in your mind. |
| ● assume your first draft of a letter/memo/report/press release is appropriate. | ● be critical of your writing style and be prepared to edit and improve a first draft. |

# Section 4

---

# Accessing and Using Information

## Objectives

By the end of this section you will be able to:

(a) maintain an appropriate library of reference books
(b) use written references effectively
(c) decide which research methods should be used to obtain information
(d) conduct a research interview effectively
(e) use a range of critical thinking skills
(f) apply a logical approach to problem solving and decision making.

# Chapter 10

## Information Gathering

Part of any secretary's job involves information gathering. This may involve:

(a) extracting relevant information from existing files or from reference books
(b) collecting data or information from other sections and departments
(c) accessing information from appropriate external organisations, agencies, etc in relation to meetings, conferences, travel.

Information gathering is the process of:

(a) collecting,
(b) selecting and
(c) recording

facts.

As you become proficient in these information gathering tasks you should be able to help your manager in some of his or her more ambitious research activities. The more heavily you become involved in researching information, the more you will find that you need to develop highly critical thinking skills. Information gathering is covered in this chapter and thinking in the next one.

# Facts — data and information

Managers require meaningful facts to make decisions. A definition of the word "information" is "meaningful facts". The facts have been put together in a way in which they can make sense to the reader or user.

Many of the facts you may be collecting for your manager have already been collected and analysed by someone else. For example you may be asked to find:

(a) a graph showing the trends in sales of a product
(b) a report outlining an investigation
(c) a published booklet on a given topic.

In other cases you may be asked to collect "data". This is unprocessed information that has not been made meaningful. For example, you may be asked to obtain:

(a) figures on the number of absences in the past year
(b) numbers of sales of a product over a given period.

Your role will probably involve collecting these facts from existing documentary records or from the individuals who hold them and then recording them on paper or on disk. Your manager will use your recorded data to select those facts he or she considers relevant and then carry out his or her own analysis to "make sense" of the facts.

As your working relationship develops you may be given more responsibility in the information gathering process. Your manager may:

(a) rely on your judgement to decide what facts need to be collected
(b) allow you to select the facts which you consider are directly relevant to his or her objectives
(c) give you discretion to record facts in the most appropriate format — text, tables, graphs, charts, diagrams, etc
(d) allow you to carry out some preliminary analysis of the facts.

However, information gathering can be a time consuming activity if it is approached in the wrong way. Eagerness and enthusiasm can cause you to rush in too quickly so that you do not use the most effective and economic methods. A secretary needs to know where to find information and how to conduct effective research.

# Where to find information

## *Using reference books*

The most valuable support a secretary can give to a manager is to know where to find different kinds of information. An important requirement is to know the types of reference books which are available to help.

---

**Action**
Take time to browse through the reference section of a modern library and note the range of reference books that may help you in your work.

---

You can then begin to build up your own library of books and reference documents that relate to:

(a) general information about businesses
(b) general reference books
(c) the business sector in which your organisation operates
(d) reference books on use of English
(e) hotels and restaurants
(f) travel and transport.

You may also need to subscribe to journals which relate to your manager's specialism so that he or she can keep abreast of modern developments. It may also be useful to subscribe to a journal which covers modern office equipment.

You may want to collect a range of simple guides and booklets which relate to specific legislation (eg the Data Protection Act), services offered by government departments, (eg Guide to Exporters) or services of advisory bodies (eg various guides produced by the Advisory, Conciliation and Arbitration Service).

A library of basic reference books which most secretaries should keep in their office is shown on page 140.

## *Loose leaf files of reference material*

Publishers now produce loose-leaf folders of reference material which are updated regularly. It may be worth your organisation investing in a ready reference source such as Croner's *Office Companion*. This provides a wealth of useful information normally only found by reference to a range of other books.

### Basic reference books

Directory of Directors, (Thomas Skinner), published annually
Who Owns Whom (UK) (Dun & Bradstreet), published annually

Whitakers Almanack (Whitakers), published annually
Pears Encyclopedia (Pelham)
Who's Who (Black), published annually
Annual Abstract of Statistics (HMSO)

Registers such as the Medical Register or professional directories such as the Travel Trade Directory.

The Oxford Dictionary (Oxford University Press)
Roget's Thesaurus of English Words and Phrases (Penguin)
The Complete Plain Words (Penguin)
Dictionary of Abbreviations (Dent)
Black's Titles and Forms of Address: Guide to Correct Usage (Black)

AA Hotels and Restaurants in Britain (AA), published annually
Good Food Guide (Consumer's Association), published annually
ABC Railway Guide (International Ltd), published monthly
ABC Shipping Guide (International Ltd), published monthly
National Express Courier Guide

## Effective research — a logical approach

Information gathering should be approached in a systematic way. It is only when the research methods are reliable that people will place trust in the results. Initially you should check with your manager to ensure that you are using appropriate methods and your manager may want to discuss each stage of your research with you. Gradually you will be capable of working on your own initiative and your manager may allow you scope to use this initiative.

## Check your terms of reference

### Check objectives

Although the overall purpose of information gathering is to aid decision making, the more specific objectives for research may be to:

(a) put a situation facing a manager into context
(b) help him or her to decide on a course of action
(c) help him or her to evaluate the success of a previous decision or course of action.

Always check your manager's specific objectives, ie what information he or she wants and how he or she intends to use it. If you neglect this stage, you may waste your time and energy collecting irrelevant facts. Clear objectives become the yardstick against which you can evaluate the suitability of the facts you are collecting.

Check whether there are other specific terms of reference for your research. These may be:

(a) time deadlines
(b) monetary constraints
(c) security issues or matters of protocol.

## Determine your sources

Determine (and agree) the sources from which you can obtain relevant facts. Your sources are likely to be:

(a) Secondary, ie material already published inside or outside your organisation —
  (i)   internal company files, manuals, brochures, reports, etc
  (ii)  externally published statistics, reports, journals, year-books, directories, books, etc

(b) Primary, ie first hand research which includes —
  (i)     observation — watching behaviour
  (ii)    surveys — using written questionnaires
  (iii)   interviews — face to face or by telephone.

Since secondary sources are usually easier and cheaper to use, the normal practice is to start your research using existing published material and then supplement this from primary sources if necessary.

## Gathering information

The physical activity of gathering information requires a range of other skills which you should already possess:

(a) reading
(b) note taking
(c) listening
(d) speaking
(e) using the telephone and
(f) being assertive.

## Recording information

Your manager may give you specific instructions about the way you record information. If so, you will obviously have to follow these guidelines. If the discretion is left to you, then you will need to give careful thought to:

(a) *what* you record — you should be selective and only record the information directly related to the objectives of the research
(b) *how* to record the information — you will need to choose whether to produce —
  (i)     a clear set of notes
  (ii)    a report.

You may also have to decide whether graphical representation is appropriate.

## Presenting facts visually

(a) *Line graphs*

These are useful for showing trends over a period of time. A simple line graph will have two axes — the horizontal axis showing the timescale and the vertical axis showing the quantity or value. Multiple line graphs, using the same axes, can be used to show contrasting trends.

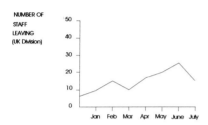
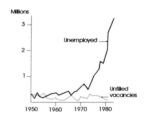

*Simple line graph showing number leaving employment in one division of an international company.*

*Multiple line graph comparing unfilled vacancies with number unemployed*

(b) *Bar charts*

Bar charts are often used to compare total quantities at different points in time or under different classifications. They can be simple or compound and can be drawn vertically or horizontally.

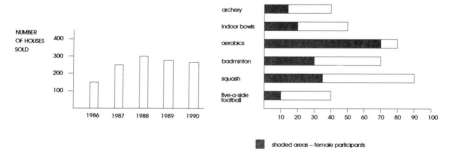

*Simple vertical bar chart showing number of houses sold.*

*Compound horizontal bar chart showing use of various recreation facilities.*

143

### (c) *Pie chart*

A pie chart is a way of showing proportions or the relationship of parts to a whole. The circle is divided into segments showing in what proportion the parts make up the whole.

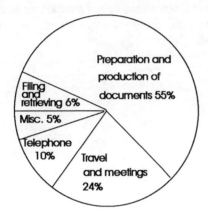

*Pie chart to show the proportion of a secretary's time spent on various duties*

### (d) *Pictograms*

If broad trends need to be shown pictionally, a pictogram can be used. A picture of the item is shown representing hundreds (or thousands) of that item. A part picture indicates smaller figures. It can be more useful than a bar chart when impact on a mass audience of varying levels of intelligence is needed.

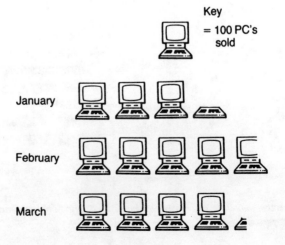

144

## (e) *Organisation charts and balloon diagrams*

Both of these can show relationships between people in an organisation. The organisation chart can be used to show the formal authority relationships down and across the organisation. The balloon diagram is useful for showing the frequency or level of communication between a number of people in a department or section.

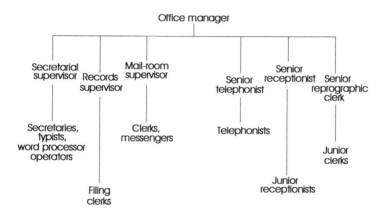

*Organisation chart*

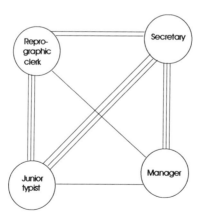

*Balloon diagram*

(f) *Gantt charts*

These can be useful to record the progress of a task or project against the original plans. The top line shows the planned timescale while the bottom line shows the actual time taken.

| | | M | T | W | Th | F | M | T | W | Th | F | M | T | W | Th | F |
|---|---|---|---|---|---|---|---|---|---|---|---|---|---|---|---|---|
| Project A | Plan | ▬ | ▬ | ▬ | ▬ | ▬ | ▬ | ▬ | | | | | | | | |
| | Actual time | ▬ | ▬ | ▬ | ▬ | ▬ | ▬ | ▬ | ▬ | ▬ | ▬ | ▬ | ▬ | | | |
| Project B | Plan | | | | | | | | | | ▬ | ▬ | ▬ | ▬ | ▬ | ▬ |
| | Actual time | | | | | | | | | | ▬ | ▬ | ▬ | ▬ | | |

(g) *Flow charts*

These are used to show the stages in a procedure including points at which critical decisions need to be made. Normally a flow chart records the procedure using simple phrases and yes/no decisions but it is possible to show a flow chart using illustrations if there is a language barrier. There is an example on page 147.

## Conducting a research interview

You may have to use this method of research to obtain information on:

(a) attitudes
(b) behaviour
(c) opinion or ideas

as well as facts.

There are  few guidelines which you need to follow if you are to handle this kind of encounter effectively.

(a) *Preparation*
    (i)    Know what kind of information you need.
    (ii)   Prepare a structure for the interview, including the number and type of questions.
    (iii)  Prepare yourself — appearance, assertiveness, ad opt a positive attitude.

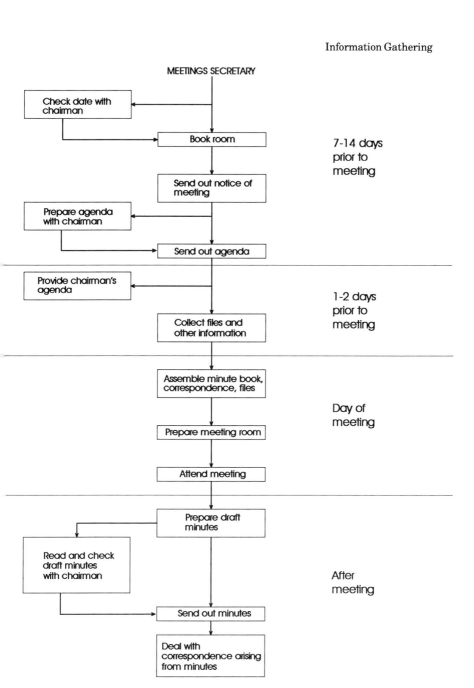

*Simple flow chart for scheduling a meeting*

## Types of question to use in research interviews

| Types of question | Purpose | Difficulty |
|---|---|---|
| Closed (call for yes/no answers) | To confirm facts<br>To limit a person's talking | Interviewer has to work hard at designing the correct range of questions |
| eg Do you sponsor sporting events? | | |
| Open | To establish a rapport<br>To explore back-ground information<br>To explore attitudes<br>To encourage a person to talk | They may open up long, rambling explanations |
| eg What events do you sponsor? | | |
| Probing | To search in more depth<br>To secure more details | Need to be phrased with tact so as not to offend or appear "nosey" |
| eg The sponsorship of athletics sound every interesting. Could you tell me a little more about what form your sponsorship takes? | | |

## Types of question to avoid in research interviews

| Types of question | Reason for avoiding it |
|---|---|
| Leading question | It indicates the answer you want and therefore does not produce an honest, objective answer |
| eg Don't you agree that sponsoring hunting events is wrong? | |
| Complex, multiple questions asked together | They confuse and mislead the individual |
| eg: Who will be receiving your sponsorship next? Will it be this year or longer? How much money will be involved? | |

(b) *Conduct of interview*
- (i) Control the direction and pace of the interview but do not dominate it.
- (ii) Ask suitable questions (see table opposite ).
- (iii) Use simple, direct language
- (iv) Observe body language to detect signs of uncertainty, annoyance, anxiety or deception.
- (v) Remain polite (even if you do not get the information you wanted!).

## Survey by questionnaire

The overall design of a survey and analysis of the results is unlikely to be the sole responsibility of a secretary. Surveys need very careful construction to ensure that the sample taken fully represents the overall population.

Also, statistical techniques may be involved in analysing the results. However, a secretary may become involved in the design of the questions and the administration of the questionnaire so it is as well to be aware of some of the requirements.

(a) *Design of questionnaire*
- (i) People do not like to spend time filling in lengthy questionnaires so the number of questions should be kept to a minimum.
- (ii) Where possible, closed questions which allow for a yes or no answer should be used. Where more open questions are asked, a range of possible answers should be provided, with boxes to tick — it is far easier to analyse the answers afterwards.
- (iii) Leading or multiple questions should be avoided.
- (iv) Each question should be clear with one possible meaning only.
- (v) Questions should be placed in a logical sequence for the person completing the questionnaire.
- (vi) Check that every question used contributes relevant information to the objective of the survey.
- (vii) If it is to be posted or delivered to participants, explain the purpose of the questionnaire clearly at the beginning; give an assurance of anonymity; thank the person for his or her co-operation.

# PLAY THE VALLEY OF THE KINGS BIG CONTEST
# YOU HAVE THE VOICE

**1st Prize :** A musical weekend for two at Chateau d'Artigny which includes the room, cocktails, dinner, a concert, breakfast and lunch on Sunday;

**2nd Prize :** A helicopter ride over the Chateaux for two, starting from Blois;

**3rd Prize :** A plane ride over the Loire Valley for two;

**4th Prize :** One week in the country;

**5th Prize :** A river boat ride.

In addition, there will be awarded 50 bottles of the finest wines of the Touraine region, models of the Chateaux, guides entitled "Open to the public" edited by the Caisse Nationale des Monuments Historiques et des Sites, tourist books, coupons and show tickets.

## In all, 500 prizes will be awarded by drawing !

The quality of our marketing study depends on your sincerity in answering the questionnaire. In order to be valuable, the questionnaire must be completely filled in. Please answer all the questions even if you are not staying here in the Loire River Valley. Your answers will not affect the results of the drawing. The completed questionnaire must be depositied in the box provided. Only one questionnaire per person, please. There is no obligation to purchase anything in order to participate in this contest.

A complete list of rules for the contest has been left in the hands of the office of R. and J.G. Morfoisse, auditors for the drawing on September 30, 1987.

### FREELY EXPRESS YOUR OPINION

Nationality _____    Age _____

Profession _____    Profession of spouse _____

**Are you on an :**          organised tour ☐          individual trip ☐

**Are you accompanied by :**     your spouse ☐          other family members ☐

                         your children ☐          friends ☐

**Is this your first trip to the Loire River Valley ? :**          Yes ☐          No ☐

**If not, in what year did you last visit here ? :** _____

**Are you here :**          for a weekend ☐          on vacation ☐          on a business trip ☐

                         other ☐  Specify _____

**How many nights will you be staying in the Loire River Valley ?** _____

**If you are on vacation will you be spending the greatest part of your time in the Loire River Valley ? :**   Yes ☐  No ☐

**If not, where will you be spending the largest part of your time ? :** _____

**During your stay in the Loire River Valley, what are your accommodations ? :**

                         a hotel ☐          chateau/hotel ☐          camping ☐

          home of friends or relatives ☐          your own vacation home ☐          your own home ☐

     other ☐  Specify _____          You're not staying in the Loire River Valley ☐

**Are you satisfied with your accomodations ? :**    Yes ☐    No ☐

**How did you choose your accomodations ? :**    travel agent ☐    advice of others ☐

office of tourisme ☐    travel guide ☐    by chance ☐

other ☐   Specify _____

**Where did you have dinner last night ? :**

in the hotel restaurant ☐   at another restaurant ☐   at your campsite ☐

a picnic ☐   other ☐   Specify _____

**Where are you having lunch today ? :**

in the hotel restaurant ☐   at another restaurant ☐   at your campsite ☐

a picnic ☐   other ☐   Specify _____

**What is your mode of transportation ? :**   personal vehicle ☐   rented vehicle ☐

charter bus ☐   train ☐   bicycle ☐

other ☐   Specify _____

**In all, what is your approximate vacation budget per person, per day (lodging included) ? :**

less than 200 Francs ☐   200 - 300 Francs ☐   300 - 400 Francs ☐

400 - 500 Francs ☐   500 - 800 Francs ☐   over 800 Francs ☐

**What chateaux do you plan to visit here ? :** _____

_____

**What cathedrals and/or abbeys do you plan to visit ? :** _____

**How do you prefer to visit these monuments ? :**   with guide only ☐   with guide + brochure ☐

with a native language brochure only ☐   accompanied by a cassette ☐   on my own ☐

other ☐   Specify _____

**What are you looking for when you visit a chateau ? :**

the pleasure of strolling in the setting ☐   the lawns and gardens ☐   the architecture ☐

the lifestyle of the times ☐   a lesson in French history ☐   the art ☐

the furnishings and decor ☐   other ☐   Specify _____

**In the chateaux, are you going to also see ? :**   the museum ☐   the expositions ☐

sound and light shows ☐   other shows ☐

**In addition to the present hours of operation, would you prefer that the chateaux also be open :**

between noon and 2:00 pm ☐   up until 8:00 pm ☐   until midnight ☐

**Do the entry fees to the chateaux seem reasonable ?**   yes ☐   no ☐

**Have you any other suggestions or comments concerning your visit to this region (hospitality, lodging, tourist information, chateau visits, informational signs, etc...) ?**

_____

_____

_____

_____

_____

**Be sure to complete for the drawing :**

**Name (last name first)** _____

**Complete address of your permanent residence :**

_____

_____

**DO NOT FORGET TO DEPOSIT YOUR QUESTIONNAIRE IN THE APPROPRIATE BOX ! THANK YOU.**

Imprim Info TOURS

There is an example of a soundly constructed questionnaire on page 150–51.

(b) *Administering a questionnaire*

If you are asked to conduct a questionnaire by approaching people personally for answers, you should:

(i)   ensure that you follow the instructions you are given concerning the choice of people to be questioned

(ii)  always ask politely for the person's co-operation in completing the questionnaire

(iii) read the questions clearly so that they are not faced with the embarrassment of having to ask you to repeat them

(iv)  do not lead a person into an answer by revealing your own preferences through placing emphasis on particular words

(v)   take care to fill in the questionnaire accurately and fully

(vi)  thank the person for his or her co-operation at the end.

So far, this chapter has dealt with some of the basic aspects of information gathering. The quality of your research will depend heavily on your ability to think logically. Critical thinking skills are covered in the next chapter.

# Chapter 11

## Thinking Skills

Unfortunately some secretaries are still viewed in terms of their ability to bring a touch of glamour into the office combined with some practical skills, rather than their ability to use intelligent thought processes. Yet effective personal assistants need a range of thinking skills as comprehensive as those of managers to enable them to solve problems and make decisions.

Your ability to use a range of thinking skills will certainly help to determine whether you progress within your chosen career.

If you look at the word "think" in a dictionary or thesaurus, you will find a long list of words such as believe, conceive, conclude, consider, determine, estimate, imagine, judge, reason, recollect. These show the range of thinking processes which we can apply in any situation. Some the these are more difficult and complex than others.

## Range of thinking skills

(a) *Simple thinking skills*
    (i)    acquiring knowledge
    (ii)   retaining and recalling knowledge.

(b) *More complex thinking skills*
   (i)    understanding information
   (ii)   applying knowledge and understanding.

(c) *Highly complex thinking skills*
   (i)    analysing
   (ii)   evaluating.

## Simple thinking skills — retaining and recalling information

These skills are the ones which are used regularly in daily routines at work — the ability to retain and then recall facts. A secretary needs to build up a large mental file of information about the organisation, the manager and his or her work, and his or her own work. A manager will often rely on the secretary's ability to recall information appropriate to a given situation (facts relating to who, what, when, where, etc).

## More complex thinking skills — understanding and applying knowledge

Since a secretary's job involves relating to other people, it is not merely necessary to be able to recall facts but also to understand fully those facts so that they can be used in new situations. For example, if a secretary fully understands the information he or she has absorbed, he or she will be able to:

(a) explain office procedures clearly and logically to a new secretary
(b) compare the characteristics of two comparable photocopying machines
(c) describe the advertising ideas of the manager to a client.

Closely allied to the ability to understand information is that of applying it. In the above situations, it is necessary to be able to select the information that applies to the situation and reject that which is irrelevant.

Therefore, a secretary is constantly recognising information in order to use it in a range of different situations. It is this ability to "manipulate" or "use" information that is most valuable to a manager if he or she is to rely on the secretary to share the work load, particularly in information gathering or in relating to other people.

## *Highly complex thinking skills — analysing and evaluating*

Analysis is a thinking skill which allows people to:

(a) break down a situation or problem into its constituent parts
(b) think through reasons
(c) probe beyond the obvious
(d) look for relationships between pieces of information.

In using analytical thinking skills, it is necessary to ask the question "why"?

For example, rather than taking a manager's bad temper at face value, try to find out what has upset him or her. Or, in finding that two apparently comparable office machines have significant differences in price, probe more deeply to find out why one should be so much cheaper. People skilled in analysis look for evidence to support general statements.

Evaluation follows from analysis. This is the ability to judge or decide. Having sought evidence, looked for reasons and probed beneath the surface, it is possible to look at the total situation and come to a valid conclusion.

Once the manager is reassured of the secretary's analytical and evaluative thinking skills, it is likely that more important decision-making may be delegated. Therefore, it is necessary to demonstrate an ability to use the full range of thinking skills.

# Using thinking skills in information gathering

You will need to use the full range of thinking skills if you are given full responsibility for researching a situation or problem. You will be involved, not just in collecting facts, but in determining whether the facts can form the basis for a sound decision. There are many ways in which facts in reports, tables of statistics or books can be presented which make their value doubtful. It is necessary to be aware of these when making judgements based on other people's facts.

For example, information is unsound because:

(a) the words or phrases used have more than one interpretation
(b) vague rather than precise words have been used (eg few, many, limited, very)
(c) a biased rather than objective selection of facts has been made (eg the writer only presents the figures or information that supports his or her ideas)
(d) conclusions (particularly in reports) do not follow from the facts given
(e) conclusions drawn from surveys are invalid because the survey was based on an unrepresentative sample or because the sample size was not large enough
(f) personal opinion or ideas (value judgements) have been introduced into reports which cannot be deduced from the facts
(g) emotive language has been used to cloud the facts.

You also need to ensure that the same faults do not appear in your own evaluation of a situation. In order to come to a valid evaluation of a situation or problem you must:

(a) not accept evidence at its face value but look for the underlying facts
(b) not make assumptions from inadequate evidence
(c) examine carefully the arguments presented by other people to determine the difference between fact and opinion.

# The role of creative thinking at work

Before leaving the subject of thinking skills it is important to mention creative thinking. The most apt words to define "creative" in this context are "imaginative" and "original".

Creative thought is generating ideas. While much of the day to day routine requires the kinds of thought process outlined in the previous sections, there are times, particularly in decision making, when originality of thought is important.

To some extent creative thought goes against the concept of organisation at work because it involves challenging existing rules, procedures or processes and suggesting something new. It is an important input in problem solving when contemplating possible solutions to problems before the more logical deductive thinking skills are used to examine the feasibility of such solutions. In decision making, creative thought is often needed to generate several options, each of which can then be systematically examined by more logical thought processes.

Individuals vary in their ability to generate ideas. Most of us are conditioned to evaluate one idea before generating another. This often means that the brain becomes diverted from developing a quantity of ideas. A technique has been developed to counteract this tendency. It is known as brainstorming.

# Brainstorming

The overall purpose of brainstorming is to encourage as many ideas as possible, no matter how extreme, without any censorship of the value of the ideas. The technique is most successful when a small group is involved.

The rules of brainstorming are as follows.
(a) A leader must be appointed to explain the rules and to ensure they are obeyed.
(b) Ideas need to be recorded on a board, flip chart, piece of paper, cassette tape, etc with no vetting by the person recording them.
(c) The objective of the decision or the nature of the problem must be identified.
(d) The group is encouraged to create as many ideas as possible.
(e) There must be no criticism of any idea by word, body language or sound.
(f) "Freewheeling" is encouraged — the wilder the idea the better.
(g) "Piggybacking" (building on another person's ideas) is encouraged.

Once a quantity of ideas have been generated more logical thought processes can be applied by:

(a) establishing some criteria by which to assess the ideas
(b) evaluating each idea against the criteria to produce a short list of possible ideas.

Some ideas may then need further investigation to determine whether their it is feasible to implement them. Another possibility is to brainstorm the ideas negatively, ie select each idea and identify all the objections to it.

It is possible to adapt group brainstorming techniques to individual use. You can practise this as part of your problem solving or decision making skills (see Chapter 11).

Allow your mind to wander freely and generate as many ideas possible, however improbable, illogical or emotional they seem to be and record them quickly on paper or screen. Do not develop any of them until your mind is totally devoid of ideas. Only then do you apply your other logical thinking skills.

---

### Action

It is useful to warm up to a serious brainstorming session by a "silly" session. For example, you might give yourself five minutes to think of as many uses of the stapler as you can.

Now apply brainstorming to the situation outlined below.

You are arranging an important conference on behalf of your manager. The conference is about the various export opportunities to eastern Europe for manufactured goods and for commercial services. You want a snappy "title" for the conference which symbolises this theme. Brainstorm to produce the best idea.

You can try this by yourself or as a group.

---

Once you have mastered critical and creative thinking skills you are ready to apply these to a logical framework for approaching problem solving and decision making.

# Chapter 12

## Problem Solving and Decision Making

For all those with responsibilities for making decisions at work the ultimate judgement is whether they make the right decisions to suit the situation with which they are faced. Decisions have to made daily, some in consultation with other people and others alone.

Some are one-off decisions; others are routine. For example a secretary probably has to make decisions about:

(a) whether to make an extra appointment for his or her manager
(b) which office furniture or equipment to order
(c) what task to undertake first at the beginning of the day
(d) who is the best candidate for the post of office junior
(e) where to book dinner for his or her manager and a client
(f) when to bring in the coffee during a rather acrimonious meeting.

### Intuitive and systematic decision making

Many people make decisions intuitively; that is, they make them according to how they *feel* at the time without going through any reasoning process. Whether this approach is used by a manager or a secretary, it is essentially a reactive approach to problem solving and decision making. The person is only reacting to the superficial needs of the moment.

This chapter will help you towards developing a more logical and systematic framework for all your own decision making. If you can apply this approach it may also help your manager to be more systematic in the way he or she tackles problem solving and decision making. This does not mean that every decision requires hours of agonising mind bending or heart searching. With some routine decisions you may go through the process in a few minutes; other more difficult problems and decisions may take hours or days.

However, once you start to apply a logical framework to all your problem solving and decision making you will find that it soon becomes a good habit. We will start with the process of problem solving as many more complicated decisions require you to solve problems first.

# Problem solving

Problems are such because they create difficulty and doubt. They are open-ended situations with a range of possible answers and finding the right answer requires thought.

The other difficulty in problem situations is that there is never enough information to work with to be absolutely certain that the solution is right. It is for these reasons that a framework on which to base reasoning is needed. You will also need to use the full range of thinking skills.

You will find that to deal with problems effectively you need a combination of:

(a) knowledge: relevant to the problem situation
(b) skills: thinking skills, information gathering skills and, in many cases where consultation is involved, a range of communication and interpersonal skills
(c) judgement: using your more complex thinking skills of analysis and evaluation,

as well as a framework for dealing with them. However, whenever possible, problems should be avoided by anticipating when situations may be becoming difficult. A problem seems far worse when you are unprepared for it. However, in many problem situations which face you there are likely to be indicators that a problem is developing. If you can diagnose problems before they get out of proportion you can solve them quickly and easily. You can detect the build up of problems by:

(a) monitoring the work in your office to identify when things are not going as planned
(b) listening to your manager and other employees to identify any anxieties about their work, their relationships, etc
(c) observing other people's behaviour — potential problems are often highlighted by inconsistent or unusual behaviour.

Once you have identified a problem then there is a logical sequence to go through for solving it.

1. Define the problem
↓
2. Plan the investigation of the problem
↓
3. Carry out an investigation into the problem
↓
4. Analyse the information about the problem
↓
5. Choose the best solution to the problem
↓
6. Implement the solution
↓
7. Monitor the situation
↓
Has the problem been solved?

## 1. Defining the problem

It is usual to find that, once a problem is examined it is no longer a single problem. It is necessary to think very carefully about:

(a) any side issues or subsidiary problems
(b) what information or resources are needed to solve the problem
(c) what constraints may affect the solution to the problem such as time, money, materials, regulations, etc.

## 2. *Planning the investigation*

This stage involves:

    (a) identifying potential solutions to the problems
    (b) identifying the required information, usually relating to —
        (i)     the causes of the problem
        (ii)    the consequences if the problem is not resolved
        (iii)  each potential solution.
    (c) deciding how to obtain the information —
        (i)     from whom,
        (ii)    when,
        (iii)  where.

## 3. *Carry out an investigation into the problem*

This stage involves

    (a) physically gathering information
    (b) selecting information relevant to the problem and the solutions
    (c) recording the information in a suitable format.

## 4. *Analyse the information*

This stage involves:

    (a) looking for trends or relationships between various facts
    (b) establishing the criteria by which to make the final choice of solution
    (c) examining the benefits and limitations of each solution in relation to the criteria.

## 5. *Choosing the solution*

As a result of stage 4 it will be found that:

    (a) one solution is preferable to the others. This should be the choice
    or

(b) two solutions match the criteria equally — if the difference between them is as marginal as this, a coin can be tossed to make the choice or

(c) no solution matches the criteria. If this is so then it may be necessary to go back to see if the problem was defined carefully enough or whether the investigation was appropriate.

## 6 & 7. *Implementation and monitoring*

The only proof that the choice was correct comes after the solution has been implemented. This is why it is necessary to check to see if the answer actually solved the problem.

If the problem solving process does not follow the logical steps outlined above, it is likely that an ill-chosen solution to a problem will merely create more problems.

It is also important in problem solving to learn from previous experiences. The same processes are involved in all problem solving but it is impossible to transfer a solution from one problem conveniently into another situation. Each situation must be treated individually. By all means use previous knowledge and skills but make sure that each solution is feasible in its particular context.

# Decision making

Problem solving and decision making are closely allied. Problem solving often has to take place before a decision can be made. Stage 5 of problem solving actually involves making a decision — a judgement. All decisions carry with them the risk of being right or wrong. Thus effective decision making is the process of reducing the element of risk to the minimum.

The logical processes involved in decision making and problem solving look very similar.

**Processes for decision making**

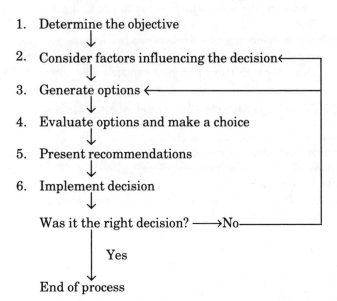

1. Determine the objective
2. Consider factors influencing the decision
3. Generate options
4. Evaluate options and make a choice
5. Present recommendations
6. Implement decision

Was it the right decision? ──→No

Yes

End of process

## 1. Determine the objective

Every decision is made to achieve something, ie there is an objective. However, it is surprising how often people rush into making decisions without clearly identifying what they want the decision to achieve.

## 2. Review the factors

List all the factors that will be important to the decision with some estimate of there relative importance. Generally there are one or more critical factors, the ones on which the success of the decision really depends. These are the criteria which *must* be met if the decision is to succeed in meeting the objective. The remaining factors can be listed in descending order of importance. This step may require more information about these factors to be collected, involving information gathering skills.

**Action**
Think for a moment of what factors may be involved in choosing
a new chair for yourself at work.

Is it really a simple decision?

For example, you are faced with practical factors to consider: how
much you can spend, which supplier you should use, which model gives
the greatest comfort, when it will be available. You may have to
consider deeper issues of relative status with other employees since
office furniture is often regarded as a status symbol and an inappropriate decision may arouse envy or resentment.

## 3. *Generate options*

Consider the various decision options for achieving the objective. Some
simpler decisions may have relatively few options and the choice
between them may be determined by reference to existing procedures
and regulations. Other decisions are more complex and both creative
and logical thinking may be involved. This is where brainstorming
techniques (see Chapter 11) may be useful. Also, remember that one
option is to do nothing — to maintain the *status quo*.

## 4. *Evaluate the options and make a choice*

At this stage an evaluation of each option and its ability to achieve the
objective and satisfy the factors which have been identified as important is being carried out. Be realistic at this stage. There may not be an
option which perfectly meets all the factors. For example, in our simple
decision of choosing a chair, the one that is the most comfortable may
also be expensive.

Reaching a decision is often arriving at the compromise which is the
best available from all viewpoints.

In complicated decisions it is often useful to produce a matrix. Across
the horizontal axis identify the various options. Down the vertical axis
identify the factors to be considered, divided into essential and desir-
able factors.

Tick boxes to identify which factors each option satisfies.

The option(s) which have the most ticks can easily be identified.

An example of this kind of matrix is shown on page 166.

## Matrix for choice between options

|  | Option 1 | Option 2 | Option 3 | Option 4 |
|---|---|---|---|---|
| **Essential factors** |  |  |  |  |
| 1 ............... | ............... | ............... | ............... | ............... |
| 2 ............... | ............... | ............... | ............... | ............... |
| 3 ............... | ............... | ............... | ............... | ............... |
| **Desirable factors** |  |  |  |  |
| 1 ............... | ............... | ............... | ............... | ............... |
| 2 ............... | ............... | ............... | ............... | ............... |
| 3 ............... | ............... | ............... | ............... | ............... |
| 4 ............... | ............... | ............... | ............... | ............... |

## 5. *Make recommendations*

In some decision making the secretary will have authority to implement the decision he or she makes. This will apply to the more routine, day to day decisions. In the case of more complex decisions, it is likely to be necessary to convince the manager that a decision is right.

It may even be necessary to convince a group of people that they should adopt a decision. This means becoming involved in the skills of oral reporting.

The basic rules here are:

(a) consider the audience in determining how to make a recommendation. This will involve determining:
  (i)   what they already know
  (ii)  what they need to know
  (iii) what they might like to know
  (iv)  what should be said
  (v)   what should be presented in visual display
  (vi)  what should be given as a written document.

(b) devise a logical framework for presenting recommendations. Essentially, this is likely to be:
  (i)   the objective for the decision
  (ii)  the factors which were considered important

(iii)   the options available
(iv)   the decision which was made and why
(v)    the request for approval of the decision.

## 6. *Implementation*

Whether implementation is directly the responsibility of the secretary or that of more senior people it will require planning to ensure that it is conducted smoothly and then monitored to ensure that the decision actually achieved the objective.

The implementation of many of the more complicated decisions at work involve change and we are all remarkably resistant to this. Therefore anticipate that some decisions, even though they are right for a job, section or organisation, may present problems for other people. It will be necessary to foresee these and be prepared to use the problem solving process.

Many management courses and books stress the importance of a logical approach to problem solving and decision making. Very little emphasis is placed on these skills for other employees.

Yet a logical approach at all levels within the organisation can bring productivity benefits.

# Consultation and decision making

So far we have looked at the basic problem solving and decision making process. Unfortunately, the effects of decisions that individuals make are rarely confined to themselves. Decisions about equipment, resources, procedures, etc often involve a range of people who have their own ideas about the suitability of various options. People have ideas about how problems should be solved.

Therefore, it is always important to identify those who might be implicated in problems or affected by decisions and try to consult them about their knowledge and feelings. Too often people withhold vital information for problem solving or resist the implementation of a decision:

"Well, if they'd asked my opinion I could have shown them why their solution wouldn't solve the problem" or
"No-one asked me what I thought. They just expected me to do what I was told."

Asking other people can provide vital information relevant to a decision or, at the least, an indication of how they might react to a particular decision. This is valuable information in its own right. If you like to be consulted in decisions made by your manager, junior staff may like to be consulted in decisions made by you.

## Accessing and using information

| *Do not* | *Do* |
|---|---|
| • appear ill-informed by not knowing where to find information. | • become familiar with appropriate reference books. |
| • rush into information gathering until you have planned your approach. | • adopt a logical approach to researching information. |
| • allow yourself to be regarded as someone without the ability to think for yourself. | • demonstrate the ability to use the complete range of thinking skills. |
| • confuse occasions when you need to use creative thinking skills with those when you need to use a more systematic approach. | • allow yourself to use creative thinking skills when the occasion suits this approach. |
| • use a reactive approach to problem solving and decision making. | • follow a logical framework for solving problems and making decisions (except when brainstorming is appropriate). |

# Section 5

---

# Managing the Office Work Load

## Objectives

By the end of this section you will be able to:

(a) identify your own time wasting faults
(b) plan the work of the office and establish priorities in your workload
(c) organise resources to get work done efficiently
(d) control work carried out within the office to ensure that plans are met
(e) practise some basic self-organisation techniques to contribute towards greater efficiency
(f) identify causes of stress and some ways of reducing it.

# Chapter 13

## Identifying Time Wasting and Inefficiency

"I've got too much work to do; there's just not enough time."
"Other people waste my time."
"Some days I don't feel I've achieved very much."

Have you ever said the above words or something like them? Has your manager said them? For most of us the answer is "yes". Time is a resource we tend to manage badly. There are numerous ways that we and other people can fritter away our time at work so that we constantly feel under pressure, doing urgent tasks and possibly not completing tasks by the deadlines we have been set.

This first chapter will identify some of the common ways in which secretaries may misuse time at work; it should prompt you to examine your own work behaviour and provide a means of checking how you actually use your time.

### Time wasting activities

There are some time wasting activities that are common to many people. The table below lists some of those which are most common amongst secretaries (and their managers).

**Some common time wasters for secretaries and managers**

1. No awareness of long term objectives of the job.
2. Unable to make decisions about priorities in tasks.
3. Relying too much on memory instead of using check lists, things to do lists, etc.
4. No clear office procedures for accomplishing work.
5. Being disorganised — cluttered desk, poor filing, poor use of the diary.
6. Poor delegation of tasks (assuming authority over juniors).
7. Doing too much or doing inappropriate tasks because of inability to say no.
8. Flitting from task to task and leaving work unfinished.
9. Spending too much time talking to people in formal or informal meetings.
10. Socialising too much.
11. Reluctance to try new methods which may be simpler or quicker.
12. Lack of self-discipline.

# Assessing your own time management problem

You may like to complete the following questionnaire which makes statements relating to time management.

### Action

If you think a statement applies to you, place a tick under the "yes" column. If you do not think it applies to you, place a tick under the "No" column. Do not ponder on your answers — your first reaction is probably the true reflection of your behaviour.

1. I always have too much work to do.  *Yes*  *No*
2. I always seem to have too many jobs on the go at the same time.

3. I complain frequently about being short-staffed    *Yes*    *No*
   in the office.
4. I start a new task before finishing the last one.
5. I never find time to think.
6. Everything I do is urgent.
7. I am the only one I can rely on to do a job
   properly.
8. I spend too much time talking to people.
9. I am always sorting out other people's work
   problems.
10. I find it difficult to say no to other people.
11. I keep getting interrupted in my work.
12. I am unable to find files and documents when
    I need them.
13. I am always hunting for the message pad.
14. I forget to remind my manager about
    appointments and meetings.
15. I like to keep all work papers — they may
    be needed some time.
16. I put off doing jobs I dislike.
17. I avoid doing some jobs because they are
    difficult.
18. I always want to do a job my way.

Count up the number of ticks in the "Yes" column — the more you
have, the bigger your time management problem!

---

You can see from the above questions that time wasting can fall into
some distinct categories. These are:

(a) *Time wasting through lack of planning*
   (i)     not knowing long term job objectives
   (ii)    not establishing priorities in work, ie between important
           and routine, urgent and non-urgent, and therefore spend-
           ing too much time on routine or non-urgent tasks
   (iii)   not allowing time to think and plan ahead
   (iv)    not using planning aids
   (v)     not devising office procedures
   (vi)    not grouping similar tasks together
   (vii)   not planning efficient layout of the office.

(b) *Time wasting through other people*
This includes:
- (i)    allowing too many interruptions to work
- (ii)   not being able to say "no" when appropriate
- (iii)  spending too much time talking to other people (meetings, socialising, drop-in visitors)
- (iv)  allowing people to impose their priorities (other managers).

(c) *Doing unnecessary work*
This includes:
- (i)    doing a job by a long, laborious method (which may be enjoyable when there is a quicker, easier method)
- (ii)   not delegating more routine tasks to juniors (if applicable)
- (iii)  being too conscientious on small details that do not directly affect the overall objective of a job.

(d) *Being personally disorganised*
This includes:
- (i)    neglecting the filing
- (ii)   not using a bring forward system
- (iii)  not putting things away after they are finished with
- (iv)  having a cluttered desk and work area
- (v)   trying to memorise telephone messages.

(e) *Too self-centred*
This includes:
- (i)    always opting to do the easy, pleasant tasks first and avoiding more difficult work
- (ii)   always insisting on doing a task in a particular personal way rather than listening to advice on quicker, easier methods
- (iii)  inability to learn from mistakes.

There is also one other major area of time wasting that needs to be considered — *the ability to waste other people's time*. This can be done by:

- (a) interrupting them
- (b) trying to impose one's priorities on them
- (c) depriving them of vital information
- (d) providing information that is inadequate or inaccurate.

You will probably find that your own time wasting faults cluster around a particular source mentioned above. Now you have understood the main time wasters that can affect your work, it is time to undertake some more constructive analysis.

Once again this will be posed as a series of questions. Only you can provide the answers to them. However, if you think carefully about each one and perhaps talk it over with your manager, you should be able to start making more effective use of your time.

---

**Action**

Try to answer the following questions honesty and fully.

1. What are my work objectives?

2. What tasks in my job description contribute most directly to these objectives?

3. Am I giving sufficient time to tasks that are important to achieving my work objectives?
   If not, what types of task am I using this time for?

4. In what ways do I let other people waste my time?
   Are there particular people who interrupt my work?
   How can I limit their interruptions?

5. Am I doing tasks which really do not need to be done at all?
   If so, what are they?

6. (To be answered by secretaries with subordinates.)
   Am I doing tasks that could be done just as well (or almost as well) by one of my juniors?
   If so, what are they?

7. Am I doing anything that wastes my manager's time?
   If so, what am I doing?

8. What are the consequences of my personal time wasting for:
   (a) myself
   (b) my manager
   (c) my organisation?

---

Self-analysis of time mismanagement is an activity which needs to be undertaken at regular intervals. You may start with good intentions but it is very easy to slip into some bad habits.

While this chapter has concentrated on the negative aspects — how you can waste time — the following chapters in the section will provide more positive information.

# Chapter 14

## Planning Work and Setting Priorities

Some people confuse "being busy" with "being efficient". It is possible to fill the day with a range of activities without necessary doing the right tasks or doing any of them well. One of the most important aspects of being an efficient secretary is planning and organising work to achieve job objectives.

In the last chapter some common faults which arise from poor planning should have been identified. For example, you may recognise that you:

(a) have a tendency to do work you enjoy first and put off doing some tasks for as long as possible
(b) carry out tasks as they appear on your desk and then find there is insufficient time to do an important task properly
(c) are doing complicated tasks when you are tired and that your error rate increases.

The results of poor planning are:

(a) important jobs are not done well

(b) urgent jobs get left
(c) work is done under stress
(d) the manager may complain
(e) a flustered, pre-occupied or offhand appearance is presented to other people and therefore an efficient image is not projected.

It is therefore in everyone's interests that you learn to plan your work well.

# Setting priorities

## *Setting priorities with manager(s)*

Initially a secretary will plan priorities and workload with the manager(s). This will promote understanding of the main objectives in their work and what tasks are important to them. It is necessary to check back constantly about how they regard the importance or urgency of the task. When a secretary is more familiar with the work he or she will be able to identify priorities alone.

With increasing job confidence it is important not to lose sight of the main purpose — to help the manager accomplish his or her work. A manager's priorities are the secretary's priorities. It is too easy to start planning and organising work totally to suit one's own needs rather than those of the manager. For example, if he or she interrupts an important task with a request to do something else it is necessary to ask which job should take priority.

## *Working for more than one manager*

When working for more than one manager, it is even more important to plan time. The work of one manager may take precedence over others, because of seniority. However, it is more likely that it will be necessary to discuss the workload in the early days of a job with each manager and get them to recognise the pressures on the secretary's time and to agree a set of guidelines for determining priorities.

Ensure that there is time at the beginning and end of each day to check forthcoming events and workload and rate each manger's work in terms of urgency and importance.

# *Urgent v important*

By determining priorities, tasks which are important or urgent are separated from those which are routine and non-urgent.

## *Important*

These are tasks which:

(a) *must* be allocated time to complete
(b) contribute directly to the main functions of the secretary's job or that of the manager.

Their importance may be determined by the secretary or the manager. They may be:

(a) tasks done regularly (eg calculating petty cash)
(b) one-off tasks (eg re-organising the layout of the office).

When a task is important it is necessary to set aside an appropriate amount of time to do it properly.

## *Urgent*

These are tasks which:

(a) cannot be put off until later
(b) must be done by a specific time.

They may be urgent for a number of reasons. Some of these are obvious, eg:

(a) the manager has set the deadline or
(b) an emergency has occurred which has made the task urgent.

Others require a greater depth of thought, eg:

(a) other people's work may depend on completion of the task by a given time or
(b) there is a built-in deadline for the task (eg a time limit for a reply given in a telephone message or a letter).

Do not confuse urgency with importance. Important tasks are not always urgent. It may be necessary to plan some time to accomplish them but it is possible to determine when the most appropriate time may be. Urgent tasks can be short, unimportant tasks (eg changing the ribbon on a typewriter or printer because it will not print effectively until this is done).

If a task is:

(a) urgent and unimportant — do it immediately but do not spend too much time accomplishing it
(b) urgent and important — do it immediately and calculate how long it will take to do it properly.

If there are a number of urgent tasks:

(a) check the deadlines for each
(b) estimate the time to accomplish each,

then decide on a logical sequence for the tasks.

If there are a number of important tasks:

(a) determine how vital each one is to accomplishing the main objectives of the job,
(b) estimate the time needed to accomplish each task,

then allocate a specific time during the day for each task.

## Unexpected tasks

Plans are produced to determine how work is going to be accomplished based on the information to hand at the time. It is not a *rigid* timetable of events. It is necessary to accept that unexpected events will upset any planned programme. All good planners incorporate some flexibility in their plans so that they can adapt to meet changing circumstances.

For example, in planning your work for a day or planning appointments for your manager, try to build in some "slack" time. This allows for:

(a) the task which takes longer than estimated
(b) the unexpected job or visitor.

If there are no emergencies or interruptions, you can use your slack time for:

(a) thinking and planning ahead,
(b) doing a non-urgent task planned for a future date.

## *Trying to avoid the unexpected*

There are some actions which improve awareness of what is likely to happen in the future and therefore the ability to anticipate events. These include:

(a) checking the manager's diary and appointment book for entries he or she has made so that tasks related to these events can be completed (arrangements made, files extracted, information collated and printed)
(b) anticipating tasks which will be complicated and will take some time (eg lengthy reports) and agreeing with the manager the time it will take for the whole task to be completed (eg a gentle reminder may be necessary that a report needs typing, editing, photocopying, binding and distributing before the written draft can be used in a meeting)
(c) reminding the manager of important and urgent work of which he or she may be unaware.

So effective planning is a joint activity between secretary and manager.

# Patterns of work

As familiarity with a job grows, a pattern will emerge. Work tends to be accomplished in cycles. Some tasks may be repeated daily, others weekly, monthly, quarterly or yearly. In offices some events may be linked to the calender year while others relate to financial or academic years.

There will be fluctuations in work load. In some offices, particular days of the week are very busy. In others, a particular time of year may be hectic (eg the end of the financial year in an accounts office, peak holiday time in a travel agency).

Careful observation of these patterns enables them to be used to assist in planning. You will know when you need to carry out particular tasks and can block them into your schedule of tasks in advance.

# Using planning aids

There are various products on the market which can help to plan work. Many of these also assist in maintaining a control system over work (see Chapter 15).

## *Diaries*

A well maintained office diary is one of the most useful planning aids for recording critical events and activities. If you are involved in paper-based diaries, you will probably need to keep two:

(a) the manager's diary
(b) your own work diary.

You will need to have a brief meeting at the start of each day to compare diaries and update items.

### *The manager's diary*

It is in this diary that you or your manager will record:

(a) meetings to be attended
(b) appointments to be kept
(c) telephone calls to be made
(d) deadlines for projects or tasks

and it is vital that you consult the existing entries in this diary before committing your manager to any new activity. You will need to agree a mutual system for maintaining this diary which allows for:

(a) access at all times by both of you
(b) security of the diary and its contents
(c) sufficient detail in the entries to make sense to you and your manager
(d) every entry to be clearly written so that details cannot be misread

(e) a way of distinguishing between provisional arrangements and confirmed arrangements

(f) mutual agreement on symbols or abbreviations.

## Example of entries in a manager's diary

**JUNE 1992**

---

**MONDAY**
**22**

    11.45   Appt.  Bob Constantine Marketing Director
                  National Leisure Ltd.

    12.45   Lunch  Grand Hotel  (for 2)

    ~~15:30~~  ~~Interview~~  management trainee
              D Stoker
              (Nick Moore substituting for interview)
    16.30  Intercity to B'ham.

---

**TUESDAY**
**23**

---

**WEDNESDAY**
**24**

## *The secretary's work diary*

This diary is likely to be larger and more detailed than your manager's diary. You will need to record:

(a) your manager's appointments, deadlines, events, etc

(b) additional information and deadlines for your own role in these events, ie reminders to yourself

(c) regular activities and deadlines which relate to your own work (eg checking stationery or petty cash, annual staff review).

By consulting both diaries you will be able to schedule your work for each day. This can then be outlined on a day planner. The contrast between the diaries of the manager and the secretary are shown on page 183 and 184.

## Example of entries in the secretary's diary

**JUNE 1992**

---

**MONDAY**
**22**

Prepare agenda for J for monthly progress meeting 29.6.9— and circulate (Book meeting room 2 for 10.30 am.)

11.45   J has appt. with Bob Constantine Marketing Director of National Leisure Ltd (071 666 2489)

NB. May bring assistant. If so adjust booking for lunch.

12.45   J   lunch with Bob Constantine Grand Hotel (booking for 2)

amend booking if assistant arrives (0953 85214)

Keep J clear until   14.30 pm.

15.30   J interview with D Stoker — for management trainee

Nick Moore substituting J's — use J's office

16.30   ✓ catching Intercity to B'ham book taxi for 15.55.

### Electronic diaries

Integrated business software often incorporates an electronic diary. This enables the secretary to:

(a) scan the diary pages
(b) key in commitments
(c) block out times when a manager does not want any kind of interruption
(d) insert reminders, memory joggers, priorities
(e) access diaries of other managers (if in possession of their security password) to make appointments or to arrange meetings
(f) scan related information in databases or spreadsheets, etc while processing the diary.

## Day planner

This type of work planner is usually referred to as a "things to do today" planner (see example on page 186).

It enables the secretary to list all the tasks to be done that day, to highlight those that are urgent and important and to exercise task control by ticking off each item as it is completed. It serves the purpose of a check list. Electronic diaries often incorporate facilities for producing this form of memory jogger.

## Bring forward system

This system enables a secretary to "bring forward" items which need his or her attention or that of the manager.

To create a bring forward system, it is necessary to set aside a drawer in a filing cabinet or use a concertina file with pockets.

Alternatively, an electronic bring forward system can be used. The principle remains the same whatever method is used.

The system works by keeping notes (as reminders) to contact a client, pay a bill, photocopy a report, send out an agenda for a meeting) or *copies* of relevant documents in a "compartment" relating to the appropriate month of the year. At the beginning of a month these are re-allocated for the current month into pockets for each day.

Each morning the notes or copy documents relevant to that day are extracted for action as part of "things to do today". Therefore, items that entered the system as reminders of future events are brought forward into current planning.

## THINGS TO DO TODAY

Date:

Key U = urgent                Tick when done
     I = important

1. ........................................................ ............

2. ........................................................ ............

3. ........................................................ ............

4. ........................................................ ............

5. ........................................................ ............

6. ........................................................ ............

7. ........................................................ ............

8. ........................................................ ............

9. ........................................................ ............

10. ........................................................ ............

11. ........................................................ ............

12. ........................................................ ............

13. ........................................................ ............

14. ........................................................ ............

15. ........................................................ ............

**Action**

If you do not use a bring forward system already, you could start thinking about the types of item you could put into such a system.

## *Weekly, monthly or yearly work planners*

Wall mounted planners are available for dealing with longer periods. These are particularly helpful when working for more than one manager. There are specialist wall planners for different types of business, for recording holiday rotas, for recording the use of specific rooms, etc (Examples are shown in the specialist office stationery and equipment catalogues.)

## *Action plans*

### *Daily planning*

The method of planning activities each day is to incorporate each form of planning mentioned so far.

(a) Sort through the post and make a priority list of those items which need to be dealt with urgently. Make notes to insert into the bring forward system. Also prioritise important items that will need attention that day.
(b) Check diaries and bring forward system for other items which need to be dealt with that day.
(c) Check any items left from yesterday's "things to do" list.
(d) Compile a list of "things to do today".
(e) Discuss work in hand with the manager and amend the list of priorities.
(f) As the day progresses, cross off tasks completed and amend the remaining items in view of new information, messages, etc.
(g) Make notes in the diary and/or bring forward system of any important items relating to future events.

### *Long term planning*

If a secretary is involved in long term planning for an important event such as:

(a) organising a conference
(b) organising a training course or
(c) arranging an extended business visit

it will be necessary to produce quite an elaborate action plan. In this case:

(a) Identify the nature of the event, the resources needed, the deadlines to observe and the aspects which involve personal responsibility.
(b) Discuss the requirements with the manager and anyone else who will be directly involved so that there is full agreement on objectives, resources and timing.
(c) Analyse the total range of personal tasks and make a list of them.
(d) Arrange the tasks in a logical order.
(e) Identify tasks that are:
    (i)    concurrent (ie can be done at the same time)
    (ii)   sequential (ie one must follow on from the other).
(f) Allocate appropriate timescales to each task.
(g) Identify deadlines by which specific tasks must be finished.
(h) Work back from deadlines to allocate a starting and finishing time for each task.
(i) Note deadlines in the diary and include appropriate reminders in the bring forward system.
(j) Draw up a master action plan similar to the one shown on page 189.

# Organising manager's action

Although you may plan effectively, you may have a manager who tends to have difficulty taking action on matters at the appropriate time. It is part of your role to highlight action and act as a tactful memory jogger for your manager.

It is useful if you can develop a simple system for achieving this. This can be paper-based or on an electronic organiser. If your manager has trouble with priorities in his or her own paper work or activities, the system identified in the next action point may help.

## Action planning sheet

| Task (in order) | Task Description | Time allow-ance | Date Action | |
|---|---|---|---|---|
| | | | Started | Completed |
| | | | | |

**Action**

Use three different coloured folders which you hand to your manager for action, eg:

Use a *red* folder for all queries, reminders, etc that you think should be *dealt with that day*

Use a *yellow* folder for those items which must be *actioned within 2-3 days*

All items that are of general interest and may require *some follow-up at a later date* can go into a *green* folder.

Alternatively you can use a coding system within your electronic organiser to highlight the same kinds of feature.

# Delegation

It may be necessary to plan and organise the task performances of juniors. This involves:

(a) establishing targets for them to achieve
(b) deciding who should carry out a particular task
(c) identifying what needs to be done and giving clear instructions about
    (i)    what needs to be done
    (ii)   the quality standards they should observe
    (iii)  the timescale within which the task should be completed
    (iv)  why it is important to maintain the standards laid down.

Always ensure that the person to whom a task is delegated:

(a) has the resources to carry out the task
(b) has the knowledge and skills to carry out the task
(c) has fully understood the instructions received
(d) has an appreciation of the quality standards expected of them, eg
    (i)    speed of reply to certain letters
    (ii)   speed of answering incoming telephone calls
    (iii)  deadlines for dealing with outgoing mail.

Within your own work schedule you will need to allocate time each day to briefing juniors on their day's tasks, dealing with their queries and monitoring their performance.

If you need to give instructions to juniors which identify steps to be followed or procedures for accomplishing work, it is often helpful to provide this in the form of:

(a) check lists which they can follow step by step
(b) a flow chart which shows the correct sequence for the procedure diagrammatically.

There is an example of a flow chart identifying some of the above points regarding delegation below. There is one section missing from the flow chart — monitoring the junior's performance in undertaking the task. Control is dealt with in the next chapter.

### Example of a flow chart on delegation

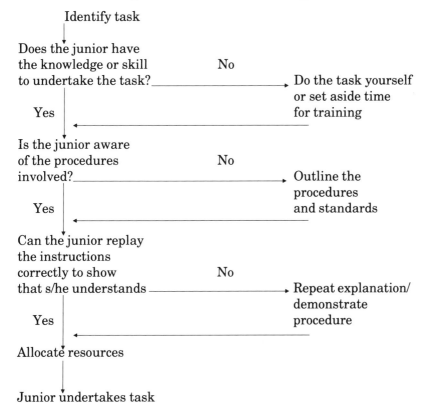

# Chapter 15

## Controlling Work

Plans and planning aids are useless without some kind of monitoring system to check whether objectives are achieved. Juniors also need to know exactly how well they are accomplishing their own tasks (whether they are achieving the appropriate objectives and standards).

## The purpose of a control system

Essentially the purpose of a control system is to:

(a) chart progress against plans
(b) enable action to be taken when problems occur
(c) give praise for doing tasks well.

The characteristics of a good control system are that:

(a) it is based on a plan; this means that a schedule, target or work standard is necessary
(b) it is possible to measure performance against the plan
(c) information about task performance can be obtained quickly so that appropriate action can be taken.

# Ways of maintaining control

## *Observation*

Once the work of others has been planned, a simple method of control is to watch what they are doing. In many clerical tasks — photocopying, filing, typing — watching juniors do their tasks or examining the results of their performance will indicate whether they are carrying out instructions in an appropriate way.

However, do note your own reactions to this method of control if your manager uses it on you. It can be annoying or even unnerving to have someone hovering over your desk or making obvious enquiries about your progress. Observation should be handled tactfully.

## *Control by progress reporting*

This is likely to be a method used between you and your manager. The purpose of a brief meeting with your manager first thing in the morning is to review orally the progress of the previous day and to plan the coming day in the light of this information. This enables your manager to control progress and change instructions as the situation demands.

You will probably use a similar system with your own juniors. You may ask them to complete simple record sheets to be handed in at the end of each day showing what they have achieved or use the morning briefing session to check this information.

## *Control by exception*

Some managers may prefer this method of control. It means assuming everything is going according to plan unless they are told to the contrary. This relies on a self-reporting system when problems are experienced or there is uncertainty about how to proceed.

It is an acceptable method of control when there is full confidence in the experience, knowledge and skills of the person completing the task. It is not a suitable method to use with new, untrained staff.

## *Automatic controls*

In some office procedures it may be possible to build in automatic controls, ie a certain course of action will come into effect if a particular situation occurs. This is the type of self-regulating mechanism built into many machines to prevent major problems occurring. For example, a paper jam in a photocopier will trigger a warning signal and shut down the operation to prevent further paper from being fed into the machine.

If you are devising office procedures with your manager you can agree that such control mechanisms can be "built into" your procedures (possibly using your bring forward system). For example, to control regular supplies of brochures for distribution to clients, you can put in a reminder to re-order immediately stocks fall to a particular level.

## Control aids

Some of the planning aids mentioned in the previous chapter can also be used as control aids.

### "Things to do today" lists

These can be used as control documents. The pre-printed forms usually provide boxes to tick once tasks are completed. Alternatively can be crossed off a check list as they are completed.

Examination of the list at the end of the day will indicate:

(a) whether urgent tasks were completed on time
(b) whether the important tasks allocated to that day were completed
(c) whether too many tasks were crowded into a day (indicated by the number of tasks left on the list).

### Bring forward system

Used correctly a bring forward system is, in itself, a control over work. It will ensure that an important event or document is not overlooked.

### Action sheet

Note that the last column on the example action sheet in Chapter 14 allows insertion of a date or time when a task is actually completed. This records progress against the plan so that adjustments can be made to ensure that deadlines are met. If it is possible to see at a glance when the schedule is slipping appropriate action (contingency plan) can be taken eg by working overtime, securing assistance from other people or, possibly, deferring less urgent tasks.

## Gantt charts

Some offices use a special chart known as a gantt chart to show the progress of a project against a plan at a glance.

It is usually in the form of a wall chart and is particularly useful for comparing the progress of two projects so that a rational allocation of resources between them can be made. An example of a Gantt chart is shown in Chapter 10 on page 146.

## Other visual planning and control boards

Visual display boards can be useful when it is necessary to show an up-to-date picture of a situation which is changing rapidly. They provide greater control over a situation and cue decisions when problems arise. This type of board is useful for:

(a) monitoring the activities of several managers
(b) controlling the timetabling and/or room allocation for meetings, training sessions
(c) ensuring no two key managers in the office are on holiday at the same time
(d) checking on the location of key people at any point in the day.

Boards can be bought off the shelf for general use or specially devised for particular applications. Whatever type of board is chosen (paper, magnetic white board, peg board) it should:

(a) enable information to be updated quickly and easily
(b) be located where the people who need to use it have easy access
(c) have an explanatory heading
(d) have a simple key which clarifies the coloured strips, symbols or shapes used on the board.

# Options available if plans are not achieved

If you find, when monitoring performance, that plans are not being achieved, you will need to use your problem solving and decision making skills to determine what action to take.

Essentially there are three forms of action:

(a) you can choose to do nothing at all. This may be the only action in a "one off" event which goes wrong
(b) adjust the plan so that you can still achieve your original objectives but by different means
(c) adjust the way tasks are being performed so that the plan can be followed.

Good planning and control should enable you to manage your work load with the minimum of stress. However, the next chapter will consider the issue of work stress and what can be done to alleviate it.

# Chapter 16

## Self-organisation and Coping with Stress

Stress is a word often used at work. Generally, the word means "feeling under pressure". Sometimes it is positive — the pressure creates an enjoyable challenge. More often it is negative — the feeling of pressure leads to anxiety, tiredness and an inability to cope. This chapter concentrates on negative stress and what steps can be taken to reduce the pressure.

### Identifying causes of stress

Chapter 13 identified some of the time wasting faults which contribute to a feeling of being under pressure from a self-induced workload or from the impositions of other people.

Other common causes of negative stress are:

(a) being uncertain about one's job role
(b) having different views about one's job role from those of one's manager
(c) not being assertive in difficult situations
(d) too many people imposing their expectations in terms of use of one's time and energy

   (e) going through a period of change at work:
      (i)    in structure
      (ii)   in people
      (iii)  in work procedures
      which creates doubt, uncertainty, or resentment
   (f) feeling isolated with problems
   (g) having problems outside work life which affect performance at work.

In the last case, some of the events in personal life which are considered most stressful include:

   (a) going through a change in family circumstances (unpleasant or pleasant) such as bereavement, divorce, separation, marriage, giving birth
   (b) moving home
   (c) holidays
   (d) money problems.

# Reactions to stress

We all react slightly differently to stress and have particular situations or events that we find stressful. In part, the way we react to stress is derived from our personality. Some people appear to react very positively to pressure — they literally thrive on it. Others find undue pressure creates negative reactions.

We also vary in the kinds of situation we find give rise to negative stress. For example, someone with an introverted personality is likely to find coping with other people stressful, while the extrovert will find rejection or lack of contact with others has a similar effect. Those who are orderly and precise will find working in a very flexible environment puts them under pressure, while the "free spirits" will find they cannot cope effectively with attempts to limit and structure their thinking and activities.

It is important to note your own main causes of stress and to observe how people with whom you work react to stress. Recognition of the signs of stress enables you to deal with it in its early stages before it becomes a real problem.

## *Recognising signs of stress*

When we are experiencing negative stress, we tend to show physical, psychological and behavioural symptoms. These become progressively more marked as the level of stress increases.

### *Mild stress*

This is the level where you feel "under pressure" but in most cases you can overcome the difficulties and therefore it is only short term.
The symptoms are:

(a) disturbed sleep pattern
(b) feeling tired
(c) minor ailments (headaches, digestive upsets)
(d) irritability
(e) less tolerance of and sensitivity to others
(f) a greater tendency to being self-centred
(g) faster talking, eating and drinking
(h) concentrating on detail and routine rather than the important things in life
(i) putting off tasks or making decisions
(j) feeling less good about ourselves
(k) giving way to more negative emotions such as resentment, apathy, anger or guilt.

### *More prolonged stress*

If the tension is not relieved in the earlier stages, more serious problems are likely to develop:

(a) indulging in excesses (sleeping, drinking, eating)
(b) more severe physical upsets including backache, migraines, stomach pains
(c) intensification of any allergic complaints (hay fever, asthma, skin rashes)
(d) unreasonable concern about health,
(e) more extreme behaviour — aggressive, autocratic, rude, stubborn
(f) withdrawal from other people (witholding information, failing to communicate)
(g) talking louder and faster

(h) having difficulty finishing own sentences but anxious to interrupt other people

(i) making mistakes more frequently

(j) an inability to make decisions

(k) a feeling of losing control.

### Severe stress

In cases of severe stress, often the stage when people feel they cannot
deal with their own problems but need help from others, one may find
symptoms such as:

(a) blurred vision and feelings of dizziness

(b) difficulty breathing and severe heart palpitations

(c) severe physical orders which are stress related ulcers, heart
condition, muscular pains)

(d) withdrawal from other people into oneself — an inability to
communicate

(e) loss of control over emotions

(f) loss of self-esteem

(g) no sense of perspective.

Once you have read this list, you, in common with most people studying
stress, have probably identified that you have all the symptoms!
However, recognition of some of these characteristics as symptoms of
stress is the first stage to coping with the problem.

# Coping with stress

Essentially the answer lies in self-organisation.

*You need to be in charge of your life in order to cope effectively with
stress.*

Some positive steps are examined below:

### Detecting signs of stress

This means studying your own personality, needs and behaviour and identifying the particular work, home and social situations which create your stress. Watch for the early warning signals that you are under pressure and then *do something about it.*

## *Giving yourself a head start*

(a) *Maintain a healthy regime*
This includes a sensible approach to eating, drinking, sleeping and exercise. If you are feeling well physically you are better able to cope with the psychological aspects of stress. You need to be careful not to sacrifice your leisure time to work. A healthy balance between work and enjoyment is necessary to face pressures and to relieve the stress from them.

(b) *Try relaxation techniques*
Try experimenting with various relaxation and stress management techniques. Discover the ones that work for you and use them; this may include calming activities such as listening to music, practising yoga or releasing tension by physical activity in individual or team sports.

(c) *Develop a positive attitude*
Develop the attitude that you are in control of your life, not events and other people in charge of you. A positive attitude towards controlling your behaviour will help you use stress management techniques at work.

## *Face the causes of your pressure — do not avoid them*

Much prolonged stress is derived from avoiding rather than dealing with a difficult situation or problem. Action is the best way of coping with stress. "Living with" a problem in the hope that it will go away by itself is not a constructive coping strategy — doing something about the problem is constructive.

For example:

(a) if you are uncertain about your role or have differing views to those of your manager, talk about it rather than letting resentment fester
(b) if you find talking to or dealing with other people stressful, enrol on an assertiveness course

(c) do not concentrate on your failures (we all have them however good we are); think about your strengths and achievements too

(d) do not struggle to achieve unrealistic, unattainable objectives set by yourself or other people — it is bound to lead to failure or undue stress. Talk through objectives and agree what you are *able* to achieve.

## *Talk to others*

As you can see in most of the above examples, talking about what causes you stress is important. Once you have voiced problems, fears or resentments out loud, either to the person concerned or to a friend, it is usually easier to see a solution to the problem. Never isolate yourself when you are under pressure. A supportive group of friends, relatives and work colleagues can either help you to resolve problems or put them in perspective.

If your prolonged stress is moving into the severe symptoms, do not struggle on alone — get professional counselling.

# Self-organisation at the office

Below you will find a more precise list of hints for being better organised at work, so that you are less likely to experience work stress.

## *Planning work*

(a) *Be prepared to spend time planning* in order to save time later; time spent on planning is never wasted.

(b) *Establish priorities* in the work load. This is the way to control and provides knowledge of what can be sacrificed when the unexpected happens.

(c) *Schedule thinking time into each day,* preferably at the beginning and the end. Assess what needs to be done, plan to do it and organise resources to achieve it.

(d) *Make use of planning aids* — the diary, bring forward system, things to do lists, wall charts, etc.

(e) *Be realistic* about how long tasks will take to accomplish and build the appropriate time into the daily schedule.

(f) If, despite good time management, the workload is *still* excessive, then *talk to the manager* about ways of relieving the pressure.

## *Organising work*

(a) Always *give priority ratings to items* on a things to do list and implement the list according to these priorities.

(b) *Organise related tasks together* (eg do a batch of photocopying rather than going backwards and forwards with odd items).

(c) *Keep the work area tidy.* This enables items to be found quickly.

(d) *Clear away the papers* from one task before starting another.

(e) *Have clearly defined office procedures* (eg for dealing with the morning mail). This enables time to be used effectively and provides a framework to be used by others during holidays or illness absence.

(f) *Do not procrastinate* on unpleasant jobs.

(g) Whenever possible, *find the right time for the right job.* Try to do complicated, important tasks at your best time of working. Remember you can do the more mundane, routine jobs reasonably efficiently even when you're not at your best.

(h) *Promise yourself "treats"* at the end of a difficult task — it helps you to get the work done.

## *Controlling work*

(a) *Check progress against plans* at frequent intervals in order to anticipate problems.

(b) *Develop control systems* for monitoring the work of any juniors.

## *Preventing others from misusing your time*

(a) *Do not invite "drop in" callers in to the office.* Also examine why they feel they can interrupt work. (Are you too pleasant to them? Are you too helpful?)

(b) *Try standing up when people come into the office* and remain standing — it is difficult for them to settle for a chat in this situation!

(c) *Agree times each day with your manager when you are both "unavailable".* This provides time for priority items and thinking. People will soon learn to come at more convenient times.

(d) *Keep to the point* in dealing with other people in person or on the telephone; be courteous but concise.

(e) *Ration time*. Adopt a standard answer to the "I'll only take a few minutes of your time . . ." approach. For example, "I can spare you five minutes now or, if it needs longer, I can see you at . . ."

## Avoiding misuse of other people's time

(a) *Keep to promises on deadlines* when other people's work depends on your efforts.

(b) *Respect other people's availability and priorities*. Remember that you must accord them the same rights as you would like to enjoy yourself.

## Questioning work methods

(a) *Be self-critical about your work* from time to time (ie ask yourself the following questions):

(i) Why do I need to do this? What would happen if I didn't? If the answer is "nothing" perhaps the task is unnecessary. Perhaps it may be more appropriate for someone else to carry out the work. Talk it over with your manager.

(ii) Is there a simpler way of doing this task? If there is, then introduce/discuss the use of the simpler method.

(iii) Is this quality or degree of accuracy really necessary? Talk it over with your manager. It may not be necessary to achieve perfection.
If you have juniors —

(iv) Am I doing things that could be done just as well by one of my juniors? If so, delegate those tasks and use the time for more pro-active tasks.

(b) *Look out for new developments in technology* that may help you to do your job faster or more easily.

When you are managing your existing work load efficiently, it is likely to be time to question whether you should be remaining in your existing job or moving on in your career.

Mastery of existing work often makes people look for new challenges. The subject of your own self-development will be covered in the next section.

## Managing the office work load

| Do not | Do |
|---|---|
| ● indulge in time-wasting activities | ● analyse your own use of time and detect your own time wasting faults |
| ● carry out work on an intuitive reactive basis | ● plan your work, establishing priorities in terms of urgency and importance |
| ● make plans that are absolutely rigid | ● allow plans to be sufficiently flexible to cope with the unexpected |
| ● keep your plans in your head | ● make use of the range of planning aids available — diaries, things to do lists, bring forward systems, action planning sheets |
| ● do all the work yourself (if you have juniors) | ● delegate tasks effectively (if you have juniors) |
| ● ignore the importance of maintaining control over work performance | ● monitor your own performance against plans as well as that of any juniors you control |
| ● rely on observation as the only form of control | ● use the range of control aids to help you monitor performance |
| ● "live" with stress. | ● recognise the possible causes of stress and the symptoms likely to be shown by you and others |
| | ● take control of your life and face the causes of your stress |
| | ● practise good time management and self-organisation techniques in your office. |

# Section 6

## Self-development

### Objectives

By the end of this section you will be able to:

(a) analyse your own strengths and weaknesses in terms of knowledge, skills and personal characteristics.
(b) identify your own work goals
(c) research the opportunities for:
   (i)   training and
   (ii)  employment
   that will help you attain these goals
(d) prepare a short term and long term action plan for your own self-development.

# Chapter 17

## Self-analysis of Strengths and Weaknesses

If you are a career secretary, once you feel that you have mastered the demands of one job for some time, you are likely to want a new challenge. This is not job-hopping, it is the natural response of an intelligent mind to seek work that is demanding, interesting and fulfilling.

In order to make your job changes a worthwhile progression you need to embark on some career planning and self-development. Preferably, changes in job should not just bring you more money and/or more interesting work, they should also enable you to develop your individuality — your personality.

There are several steps towards planning your career.

(a) Decide what you want your ultimate goal to be and what might be the intermediate steps to reaching this goal.
(b) Take a long hard look at yourself now — your existing knowledge, skill and personal characteristics.
(c) Decide how you can fill the gap between now and your ultimate goal by researching the opportunities available.
(d) Plan how you will make use of such opportunities.

This first chapter will deal with the first two steps.

# Your ultimate goal

You may have given this a great deal of thought already. On the other hand, it is easy to acquire qualifications and then drift from one job to another which enables you to see the qualifications, possibly lured by the chance of better pay or working conditions.

Now is the time to make decisions. The two questions posed in this section may help you towards some important decisions.

*Do you want a job to play a dominant role in your future life?*

If the honest answer to that question is no, because your home, a sporting or artistic talent or your leisure activities will always take precedence over a job, then you have established some valuable priorities and you can organise your life around them. What is important is that you have made a conscious decision. You are likely to be happy continuing in a secretarial job where the pay, hours, working conditions and people enable you to enjoy those important aspects of your life.

However, if your answer to the question is yes because you consider a career is as important or even more important than other aspects of your life, you have to decide what type of career you want. Your work life needs a goal towards which you are progressing.

This raises the next question.

*Do you find secretarial work interesting and fulfilling in its own right?*

If the answer is yes you may be happy continuing in secretarial work but making job changes that enable you to use your skills and knowledge in more challenging situations. For example, you may assume more responsibility as a supervisor within an office.

If you were hesitant in answering yes or your answer was a firm no, perhaps you should consider careers other than secretarial work. Your own experiences with different specialist managers or professionals may indicate the kind of career move you might like. You will need to think carefully about:

(a) your strengths in terms of knowledge, skills and qualities

(b) your self-motivation — what type of needs you wish to satisfy through work (eg security, respect, status, development of your potential) because this will help to determine the kind of work you will find interesting, challenging and fulfilling.

In both cases, the next chapter may help outline some of the opportunities that exist.

Whether your goal is outside work, in secretarial work or in a managerial or professional role, you need to have the ability to achieve that objective and it must interest you enough to strive to achieve it (even when the going gets tough)!

# Analysing your existing strengths and weaknesses

If you are contemplating a job move or a change of career path, the first step is to look at what you are and what you can do at present. Once you have done this you are in a stronger position to write letters of application, complete application forms and answer questions in interviews.

The end product of your analysis should be a list of what can be termed your "marketable knowledge and skills" and your personal qualities. There are two basic techniques you can use to help you do this.

## *The creative approach*

The steps in this approach are as follows.
(a) Select the five most important achievements in your life to date. These can be in any aspect of your life — academic, practical, sport, etc.
(b) Decide what knowledge, skills or personal qualities enabled you to achieve each one. This will help you to define your strengths.
(c) You can do the reverse for your weaknesses. Select a number of occasions when you have had a sense of failure. Why did you fail on these occasions?

## Example

You may consider that passing a maths examination was a great achievement (you passed it on the third attempt!). This may say more about your personal qualities than your ability or skill. You decide you passed it eventually because of your:

(a) single-mindedness — you were not distracted by other more enjoyable activities
(b) persistence and tenacity — you were not going to give up
(c) need for self-esteem — it was important to you to be seen as numerate
(d) need for recognition — maths is a subject that most people see as important

and because you were capable of being:

(e) industrious — you worked very hard to pass
(f) orderly — you set about the paper in an organised, methodical way.

As you can see, once you start analysing an achievement you can find out a great deal about yourself.

## *Personal deduction from standard lists*

Many books, including this one, can provide standardised areas of skills and lists of personal qualities.

You can use these as "mind joggers" to help you select or determine which knowledge and skills you possess.

### *Knowledge*

(a) Look at your qualifications; these will identify some of your areas of knowledge.
(b) Consider any courses you have attended; these may have included some areas of knowledge.
(c) Consider what knowledge you have acquired by doing various jobs.

From these sources you can produce a list of your areas of knowledge.

*Skills*

The list of marketable skills shown below should help you determine those which you possess.

# Range of marketable skills

*Numerical skills*      Ability to: keep accounts; handle cash; work out measurements and quantities; perform calculations.

*Oral skills*      Ability to: give instructions; use the telephone; conduct a structured discussion; conduct an interview; participate in a meeting; deliver a presentation; sell; negotiate.

*Written skills*      Ability to: write letters, memos and reports; check and edit written material; use appropriate illustrative material to support and extend the written word; complete forms; handle paperwork.

*Visual and presentation skills*      Ability to: present numerical data graphically; design illustrative material; use appropriate layout and design for written material; present self effectively.

*Research skills*      Ability to: gather data from appropriate sources; conduct investigations and/or experiments; observe results.

*Analytical skills*      Ability to: generate ideas, interpret data; use logical methods to solve problems and make decisions; evaluate solutions to problems.

*Practical and mechanical skills*      Ability to: perceive spatial relationships; operate equipment; identify and rectify faults in equipment; construct and design; create; assemble parts; install equipment or systems.

| | |
|---|---|
| *Organisational skills* | Ability to: plan; schedule time; organise others; organise yourself; control; monitor progress; co-ordinate resources and people. |
| *Team skills* | Ability to: work constructively within a group; represent a group; lead others; give and enlist co-operation: give and take constructive criticism. |

By carrying out this activity you have identified:

(a) the skills which you possess and would like to use in your career
(b) occasions when you have used those skills (useful for answers in selection interviews).

This may help to narrow the choice of jobs which you are capable of undertaking and have an interest in doing.

---

**Action**

The best way to record your skills is to produce a three column table and head the columns in the following way.

| *Skill* | *How demonstrated* | *Preference rating* |
|---|---|---|

(a) Use this table to identify each skill you possess in column 1.
(b) Identify a work situation in which you have demonstrated that skill in column 2.
(c) Give a preference rating for each skill. For example, some skills you possess you enjoy using; others you are reluctant to use. Use a 1-5 rating scale giving a 1 to those you really enjoy and 5 to those you hate.

---

### *Personal qualities*

These are aspects of your personality that are apparent in any activity you undertake. You will have some qualities of which you are proud (your strengths) and some which you probably try to hide from other people (your weaknesses). You need to be aware of both in this process of self-analysis. Unfortunately, when scrutinising ourselves, we can believe we have certain qualities which may not be apparent to other people. The only ones that we can really count in our self-analysis are those that we know we have and which are confirmed by other people.

You could undertake the following activity to confirm your strengths and weaknesses in personal qualities.

---

## Action

1. Look at the following list of personal characteristics and make a note on a separate piece of paper of the ones you think apply to you.

| | |
|---|---|
| adaptable | imaginative |
| aggressive | independent |
| amiable | industrious |
| ambitious | introspective |
| assertive | loyal |
| assured | objective |
| calm | open-minded |
| cheerful | orderly |
| considerate | patient |
| creative | persistent |
| decisive | prudent |
| dependable | reliable |
| determined | resourceful |
| easy-going | reticent |
| efficient | self-confident |
| excitable | self-conscious |
| extrovert | self-reliant |
| forceful | shy |
| friendly | sincere |
| gregarious | subjective |
| helpful | submissive |
| honest | tactful |
| humerous | tenacious |
| | trustworthy |

2. Give the original list to someone who knows you well — a friend or a member of your family. Without revealing your own choice, ask him or her to make a note of the characteristics he or she thinks apply to you.

3. Give the original list to someone who only knows you fairly well — someone with whom you have *some* contact at work perhaps. Ask him or her to record the characteristics he or she thinks you possess.

3. Compare all three lists. Where all three agree you can be sure that you display these characteristics. Where your own and those of a close person agree, you probably display these characteristics in a relatively "safe" environment.

5. Look, in particular, for characteristics that the others have noted in you that you do not think you possess (good or bad). Think about how your behaviour might give them this impression of you.

---

# How to use your analysis

Once you have carried out this analysis you should record this information in a simple format as it will become an important reference document. Keep it in a folder together with other information relevant to work:

(a) a current copy of your *curriculum vitae* (cv) (see pages 220–1)
(b) copies of certificates and diplomas awarded for your qualifications
(c) copies of birth and marriage certificates
(d) information about your health.

There are a number of ways you can use your folder.

## *Scanning job advertisements*

If you are thinking of applying for another job, you should do it in a systematic way.

(a) Look carefully at the requirements in the advertisement.
(b) If you are attracted by the job, draw up a profile of the kind of person you think they are looking for in terms of:
  (i)    physical characteristics
  (ii)   qualifications, work experience
  (iii)  intellectual ability
  (iv)   skills and
  (v)    personal qualities.
(c) Compare this profile with your self-analysis. If there is a good "fit" between the two, then apply for the job.

## Writing letters of application

Many companies like a *curriculum vitae* to be accompanied by a covering letter of application. While your CV records the plain facts about you and your work history, the letter is your opportunity to prove that you are really suited to the advertised job. Once again, you need to go back to your strengths and relate these to the job.

Although every letter of application should be individually composed, there are some standard items. These are shown in the table below. The standard information that should appear in a *curriculum vitae* is also shown.

A letter of application should always be very positive and optimistic in tone; you should *persuade* the organisation that it must interview you.

### Content of a letter of application

| | |
|---|---|
| ● Opening paragraph: | should include a clear identification of the job for which you are applying including any reference number quoted in the advertisement, plus a statement that you wish to be considered for the job. |
| ● Middle paragraphs: | should contain a selection from your achievements, skills and qualities which show you can fulfil the job requirements. You should also explain why you want to work for the organisation. |

- Closing paragraph:      should give clear indication of when you are available for interview.

## Standard information for inclusion in a *curriculum vitae*

- Personal details: full name, address, telephone number, date of birth (statement of marital status and/or nationality is optional).

- Education: a list of secondary schools and colleges attended — with dates, recorded in chronological order.

- Qualifications: a list of qualifications obtained, the subjects, examining board/organisation, the dates and the grades — recorded in chronological order starting with GCSE/O levels, A levels, college diplomas, degrees, etc

- Work experience: identification of previous jobs with dates of joining and leaving, a brief synopsis of the main responsibilities and your reasons for leaving. You should start with the most recent job and work backwards in time.

- Interests: A brief explanation of your main interests and hobbies (but only include those that you can discuss with some depth of knowledge).

- Referees: provide the names, addresses and job titles of two people from whom an employer can seek a reference.

## *Completing application forms*

You are likely to find that some application forms for jobs have a section where you are asked to:

(a) "Record any achievements in your life which you think will contribute to success in the job."
(b) "State, in your words, why you are applying for the job."
(c) "Explain how you think that your background and experience will help you if you are offered the job."
(d) "Explain what skills and personal qualities you can bring to the job."

This section is really asking you to match your knowledge, skills and personal qualities to the requirements of the job. Your lists will prove useful here, along with the column which identifies when and where you have demonstrated skills.

## *Applying for a course*

Just as you will need your information for applying for a job, you will also need it if you intend undertaking further education or training. Your letter of application for the course will need to prove that you consider you fulfil any academic requirements for the course as well as showing that you are suited for this type of education or training.

Course application forms sometimes have difficult sections to complete which require a statement of why you consider yourself suitable to undergo the course and why you are applying to that particular college.

## *Preparing for interviews*

All interviews, whether for a job or a course, are somewhat unnerving. One of the worst fears is that you will be asked a series of awkward questions. It is therefore a good idea to anticipate some of the more difficult questions that can be asked. The ones which many people find hard to answer unless they are prepared are:

(a) "What do you consider are your strengths and weaknesses?"
(b) "What do you think you can contribute to this job?"

(c) "Why have you applied for this course?"
(d) "Where do you see yourself in five years' time?"

If you have carried out your strengths and weaknesses analysis you should be able to answer the first three questions. You can select from your strengths those that you think are going to be particularly important in doing the job or undertaking the course. In identifying weaknesses, choose those that will not prove to be too damaging to your ability to carry out the job. If you have decided your goals and priorities can carried out your action plan for self-development you should be able to deal with the last question.

Once you have gone through these analytical processes and preparation, you are ready to research the job opportunities that exist.

# Chapter 18

## Researching Opportunities

Once you have decided your goals in life and where work fits into them, you need to research the opportunities that are open to you to reach these goals. As with decision making, there are several ways of reaching a goal and you will need to decide the one that is best suited to you.

This chapter will identify some of the options to you. It assumes you already have secretarial qualifications and some work experience.

### Talking about self-development opportunities within your existing organisation

There are three ways you might seek self-development within your own organisation. You might wish:

    (a) to develop within your existing job by acquiring additional skills and taking on more responsibility
    (b) to move to a more senior secretarial post
    (c) to move away from secretarial work and acquire knowledge and skills suited to a management post.

The starting point for any of the above forms of self-development is a formal talk with your manager. This may be at your request or you might like to make use of a formal job appraisal interview if your organisation carries out job appraisal.

## *Using a job appraisal interview*

The purpose of a job appraisal interview is for a manager and a subordinate to discuss the subordinate's job performance. It is meant to be a two-way conversation in which the person being appraised has the opportunity to raise matters arising from his or her work which are of concern to him or her.

If your company has this type of interview, you should prepare very carefully for it.

   (a) Identify in what areas you want to develop. For example you might want to:
- (i) develop further an existing skill (eg improve speed)
- (ii) gain knowledge and experience of different functional areas within the organisation (eg move from sales to accounts)
- (iii) acquire new knowledge or skills (eg a new foreign language)
- (iv) take on more demanding work (eg research)
- (v) develop an aptitude for a particular aspect of work to a higher level (eg working with people or carrying out market research).

   (b) Identify how this development could be achieved. For the examples given above, this might include:
- (i) enrolling on a further education course
- (ii) changing jobs and departments
- (iii) completing an in-company short course or a further education course
- (iv) having more demanding work delegated by your manager
- (v) embarking on a long term professional qualification.

   (c) Know why you consider this self-development is important and what you ultimately want to achieve. Some possible motives for the examples above might be:
- (i) improved speed will enable you to undertake important PA work for senior management, particularly servicing meetings
- (ii) experience of a wider range of business functions will be a good preparation for a job as office supervisor

(iii)  an additional foreign language will enable you to move to a subsidiary located abroad within an international company and to be a bi-lingual or tri-lingual secretary

(iv)  you are quite happy in your existing job but having done the job for some time, you feel you are ready to take on more demanding work and be of greater assistance to your manager

(v)  you have recognised that you want to use a particular aptitude and progress from secretarial work into specialist managerial work (eg personnel management or marketing).

You will need to keep an open mind during the course of the interview. A frank talk with your manager may reveal his or her doubts about your suitability to embark on the self-development you have identified. Listen carefully to your manager's views and examine the reasons. He or she may think you are trying to achieve progress too quickly or his or her appraisal of you in your present job may reveal weaknesses in your attitude or performance. If you are not satisfied with the outcome of your talk, you can always seek the guidance of your personnel manager.

If your manager is in agreement with your ideas, then it is a good idea to draw up an action plan between you (see Chapter 19).

## *Approaching your manager*

If there is no formal appraisal system in your organisation, carry out your own strengths and weaknesses analysis, identify the kind of self-development you want and then approach your manager for an interview to discuss the subject.

# Exploring career opportunities outside your organisation

## *Deciding your career direction*

You may feel that your present organisation has no further opportunities to offer you and you will need to move to develop your career. Sometimes it is difficult to know in what direction you should move. If you are uncertain about your future direction, take time to research what is involved. You can:

(a) scan papers and journals for job advertisements that interest you and then send off for details. This should give you a clearer idea of the kind of work involved and the type of people for whom the are searching
(b) write to professional institutes for details of qualifications, entry requirements and how to become a student member
(c) send off for particulars of evening classes and training courses to find out what is involved, how much it will cost and when you will need to attend.

In other words, collect as much information as you can about possible careers before committing yourself. You will then be in a position to make a sound decision.

If you are really undecided how to progress you might find any of the following helpful.

(a) Your local further education college will have specialists in a wide range of business areas who may be able to provide information that will help you make your choice.
(b) Your local public library or further education college library will have a careers reference section where you can find directories of courses and compendiums of career opportunities as well as useful addresses.
(c) You can go to the Vocational Guidance Association or other similar career counselling services. They will give you a series of intelligence, personality and interest tests designed to highlight several careers where you would have the ability and motivation to succeed. You can look for these organisations under "Careers Advice" in the *Yellow Pages*.
(d) If there is someone you know who is already doing the kind of job you think you might like, try to set up an interview to question them about their own career. Find out how they reached their present position; what qualifications they needed; what personal qualities they have found important.

## *Researching employers*

Even if you are clear about your career direction, you need to choose potential employers with care. You need to check as much as you can about a company before attending an interview.

You should also ensure that you use any job interview to question the interviewer about the organisation and the job. After all, an interview is meant to be a two-way exchange of information not a one-way interrogation!

The kind of information you will need to know is:

(a) what overall responsibilities you will have in the job
(b) what duties the job will involve
(c) for whom you will be working
(d) what opportunities for training exist within the organisation (in-company or off-site)
(e) what support is given for training (costs, time off, etc)
(f) what opportunities for development and promotion exist within the organisation and how these are achieved (by merit, length of service, qualifications, etc).

You also need to assess whether the overall atmosphere of the organisation is one that suits your temperament. For example, if you like to contribute ideas, use your initiative and operate in a casual, relaxed environment you are unlikely to be happy in a large bureaucratic organisation with an elaborate system of rules and procedures, and where formality in dress and approach is used.

On the other hand, if you feel rules, formality and a rigid structure give you a feeling of permanence, stability and certainty, it may well suit you.

# Opportunities for secretarial work

This section will highlight some of the types of specialist secretarial work you may not have considered to date. This may give you some ideas for your own career development.

## Qualifications which can assist your career

All the secretarial examining bodies — Royal Society of Arts (RSA), Pitmans Examination Institute (PEI) and the London Chamber of Commerce and Industry (LCCI) have advanced qualifications for personal and administrative assistants. These now conform to NVQ Level 3.

You will find your local college is likely to provide courses which may suit you, including some in the specialist areas of secretarial work mentioned in the sub-sections below. Colleges provide courses on a full-time, part-time or evening basis, some lasting a year or more, others consolidated into a block of several weeks.

## Professional associations for secretaries

These associations seek to improve the status of qualified secretaries and act as a mouthpiece for all those involved in secretarial work. The main associations are:

(a) *The Institute of Qualified Private Secretaries*
If offers advice to anyone wishing to train for a secretarial career.
(b) *The Association of Personal Assistants and Secretaries*
It provides a wide range of information and advice including job opportunities.
(c) *The European Association of Professional Secretaries*
This association is particularly interested in the role of secretaries throughout Europe and in promoting secretaryship as a profession.

For each of the associations, an advanced qualification and experience in a senior secretarial role is necessary for full membership.

## Specialist areas of secretarial work

Obviously it is possible to specialise as a secretary in any manufacturing or service industry, in an area of commerce or in a specific business function. This sub-section only includes a few of the many specialisms but some which you may not have considered so far.

### Legal secretaries

It is possible to take examinations to become a specialist legal secretary and belong to the Association of Legal Secretaries. You can then work in a legal practice of lawyers or solicitors. The work involves handling the correspondence and paper work concerned with civil or criminal court cases, and in matters concerning family affairs, exchange of property, etc. It is necessary to develop some familiarity with legal processes and terminology.

## Medical secretaries

If you would enjoy working in a local practice or in a hospital you might consider training as a medical secretary.

Apart from general secretarial duties you need to learn about basic human biology as well as medical terminology.

The work involves the full range of administrative support to doctors as well as reception work with patients and liaising with other medical organisations. Advice on this type of work is obtainable from the Association of Medical Secretaries, Practice Administrators and Receptionists.

## Farm secretaries

If you prefer to combine secretarial skills with the outdoor life you could consider becoming a farm secretary. Some secretaries are full-time employees on large farms or estates while others freelance round a number of different farms helping with correspondence, completion of forms and basic book-keeping. You need to learn about farming terminology, requirements of the EC and Government departments and the numerous forms they produce.

Information about this kind of secretarial work can be obtained from the Institute of Agricultural Secretaries.

## Bilingual secretaries

If you want a job which involved foreign travel with your manager or the opportunity to work in a foreign country, you might undertake a bilingual secretarial course, combining the development of secretarial skills with a fluent knowledge of a foreign language. Alternatively, you might like to add an Institute of Linguists qualification to your existing secretarial qualification.

## The armed forces

It is possible to combine use of administrative skills with a career as a member of the armed forces. The WRAC, WRAF and WRENS have opportunities in a commissioned or non-commissioned capacity. You also have the chance of working on a base overseas. Information about work in the armed forces can be obtained from regional information offices (addresses can be found in the local telephone book).

### Teaching secretarial subjects

There are opportunities to teach a range of secretarial subjects in schools, further education colleges and private secretarial colleges. Specialist qualifications for teaching these subjects are offered by the RSA and City and Guilds. However, it may also be necessary to undergo a Certificate of Education course to be a professional teacher. Initially you should enquire at your local further education college.

# Opportunities outside secretarial work

There is no reason why you should not have career expectations outside secretarial work. You may wish to progress in supervisory and managerial work in any of the business functions. Most specialist areas of management have their own professional institutes and many jobs at a supervisory level will expect you to study the first level of the professional examinations. In some organisations you may not be considered for a managerial post until you have the reached the more advanced stages in the professional examinations or have acquired the qualification.

It is therefore a good idea to contact the professional institute as a starting point for researching what may be involved in a career move. In all cases you will need to check the qualifications you will need to become a student member.

Some of the possible functional specialisms are:

(a) *Accountancy*
   The Association of Accounting Technicians
   Chartered Association of Certified Accountants
   Chartered Institute of Management Accountants
(b) *Company administration / office management*
   Institute of Chartered Secretaries and Administrators
   Institute of Administrative Management
(c) *Marketing*
   Chartered Institute of Marketing

(d) *Personnel management*
Institute of Personnel Management
Pensions Management Institute
(e) *Purchasing*
Institute of Purchasing and Supply

Some areas of business which you might like to examine are:

(a) *Banking*
Chartered Institute of Banking
(b) *Building society management*
Chartered Building Societies Institute
(c) *Insurance*
Chartered Insurance Institute
(d) *Hotel and catering management*
Hotel, Catering and Institutional Management Association
(e) *Leisure management*
Institute of Leisure and Amenities Management

The final stage in your career and self-development is to plan how you will achieve this development — action planning. This is covered in the next chapter.

# Chapter 19

## Personal Development Action Plan

Chapter 14 showed how action plans play a vital part in planning and controlling office work. They are equally important in planning personal future development. If you have attended a training course (in company or off-site) you may have been asked to complete an action plan on how you intended to apply your newly acquired knowledge or skill to work.

### Action plans for individual skills

By now you have read 18 chapters relating to skills you use as a secretary. Very few people ever achieve complete mastery of a skill; there is always room for improvement. Therefore, a good starting point in action planning is to produce one for improving personal skills in each of the areas mentioned in this book, ie developing the ability to:

(a) have an effective working partnership with your manager
(b) communicate with others in face to face encounters
(c) use effective telephone techniques

    (d) demonstrate a range of writing skills

    (e) have information gathering skills

    (f)  show a range of thinking and decision making skills

    (g) manage your work load efficiently.

For each of the above identify:

    (a) what aspects need attention

    (b) the priority you give to each aspect

    (c) how you will improve your skill

    (d) the deadline you are setting yourself for achieving the improvement

and remember to keep a space for monitoring how well you are implementing your action plan (see page 235).

# Action plan for self-development

There are several ways to accomplish this.

## Action plan for development within your existing organisation in agreement with manager

If you have agreed a course of action for your self-development with your manager in an appraisal or private interview, then you can set out that agreement as a formal development plan. One which has been used in one organisation is shown on page 236.

In this case, both the manger and the secretary signed the plan and then the manager completed the appropriate column as each aspect was actually accomplished. A copy of the plan was sent to the personnel department with the manager's request for the training needs to be met.

A formally laid out plan shows the commitment of both you and your manager to implementing the points which have been agreed.

## Individual action plan within the organisation

If your manager will not co-operate in the above way, there is no reason why you cannot set out your own action plan. It may be more difficult to achieve without co-operation (eg training may have to be done by

## Action plan for individual skills

Action plan for . . . . . . . . . . skill

| Aspects which need improvement (listed in priority order) | Method of achieving improvement | Planned deadline | Achieved (insert date) |
|---|---|---|---|
| | | | |

# Action plan for long term self/career development within your organisation

## Personal development plan (confidential document)

Name:

Job title:

Date job commenced:

**(2) Recommended Method of Meeting Need**

NOTE: Please tick the appropriate column(s) of section 2 and indicate the degree of urgency by using one of the following key letters.

- i - Immediate (needed at once)
- s - Short-term (needed within next 3 months)
- m - Medium-term (needed within next year)
- l - Long-term (needed within next 3 years)

This section to be filled in when recommended training completed

| No. | (1) Area of Training Need | On-site job | Reference material | Internal short course | External short course | External course for qualifications | Open learning | (3) Further details of recommended training | (4) Training provided | Date Completed |
|---|---|---|---|---|---|---|---|---|---|---|
| 1 | | | | | | | | | | |
| 2 | | | | | | | | | | |
| 3 | | | | | | | | | | |
| 4 | | | | | | | | | | |
| 5 | | | | | | | | | | |
| 6 | | | | | | | | | | |
| 7 | | | | | | | | | | |
| 8 | | | | | | | | | | |
| 9 | | | | | | | | | | |
| 10 | | | | | | | | | | |

Agreed between _____ (signature of manager) and _____ (signature of employee)

Date produced: _____

evening course or during holiday time). You may find this will affect your methods for achieving your plan and for your timings of the various stages.

## *Action plan for a career move*

This will have identified the various stages you will need to accomplish to achieve your ultimate goal, with estimates of when you hope to accomplish each stage. Your action plan will probably start as a check list similar to the one shown below.

(a) Carry out a strengths and weaknesses analysis.
(b) Decide what career move to make. If in doubt, seek guidance from professionals.
(c) Research job opportunities in your chosen career to determine the qualifications, experience, skills and qualities generally required and to relate these to your own profile.
(d) Confirm it is still an appropriate career move to make.
(e) Research the qualifications needed in the new career and the level of qualification needed to enter it at the supervisory level.
(f) Research the organisations that provide training for the qualifications, the mode of study and how long it is likely to take to acquire the appropriate level.
(g) Enrol on a course.
(h) Carry out some preliminary research into reputable organisations for whom you would like to work within your chosen career.

And once you are ready to make the move:

(i) Prepare your CV.
(j) Respond to appropriate advertisements.
(k) Use advertisement and any additional information sent to you to match the job requirements to your own profile.
(l) Use your list of personal knowledge, skills and qualities to complete application forms, and write letters of application.
(m) If you secure an interview, anticipate difficult questions that could be asked. Decide how you can emphasise your strengths in answering the questions.
(n) Ensure you ask questions within the interview which relate to further self-development within the organisation.

If you follow the guidelines in these last three chapters you should prepare for any major change in your job or career in a constructive, positive way so that you are aware of exactly what you will need to do to achieve your goals.

## Your self-development

| *Do not* | *Do* |
|---|---|
| just drift from job to job. | establish your ultimate goals in life. |
| assume you can do any job easily. | analyse your own knowledge, skills and qualities very critically. |
| | use your strengths and weaknesses analysis for scanning job advertisements, completing letters of application or application forms, and preparing for interviews. |
| allow anyone to deny you opportunities for self-development. | discuss your ideas for self-development with your manager and your existing organisation before leaving your job. |
| ignore points made by your manager or personnel officer which do not fit in with your own ideas. | give serious thought to any criticisms or objections to your career plans voiced by other people — they may see pitfalls you have not envisaged. |
| leave your existing job until you have fully explored the alternative job or career opportunities. | research job or career opportunities thoroughly so that you are aware of any new knowledge, skills, etc you need to acquire. |
| approach a career move in a haphazard fashion. | produce an action plan for any self-development you wish to embark upon (preferably in consultation with your manager). |

# Postscript

Whether you remain in secretarial work or decide to make a career move, I hope this book has been of assistance, and will continue to help you develop your communication and interpersonal skills. Good luck in whatever you do.

# Appendix

## Useful Addresses for Career Development

### Secretarial organisations

**Association of Legal Secretaries**
The Mill
Clymping Street
Clymping
Nr Littlehampton
West Sussex
Telephone: 0903 714276

**Association of Medical Secretaries, Practice Administrators and Receptionists**
Tavistock House North
Tavistock Square
London WC1H 9LN
Telephone: 071-387 6005

**Association of Personal Assistants and Secretaries Ltd**
14 Victoria Terrace
Leamington Spa
Warwickshire CV31 3AB
Telephone: 0926 424794

**European Association of Professional Secretaries**
Maison de L'Europe
Hotel de Coulanges
35 Rue de Francs Bourgeois
75004 Paris
France
Telephone: (1) 42 72 94 06

**Institute of Agricultural Secretaries**
National Agricultural Centre
Stoneleigh
Kenilworth
Warwickshire CV8 2LZ
Telephone: 0203 696592

**Institute of Qualified Private Secretaries**
126 Farnham Road
Slough
Buckinghamshire SL1 4XA
Telephone: 0753 864094

**London Chamber of Commerce and Industry
Examination Board**
Marlowe House
Station Road
Sidcup
Kent DA15 7BJ
Telephone: 081-309 0440

**Pitman Examinations Institute**
Catteshall Manor
Godalming
Surrey GU7 1UU
Telephone: 0486 85311

**Royal Society of Arts Examination Board**
Westwood Way
Coventry CV4 8HS
Telephone: 0203 470033

# Advice on careers

**Careers Research and Advisory Centre**
Sheraton House
Castle Park
Cambridge CB3 0AX
Telephone: 0223 460277

**National Advisory Centre on Careers for Women**
8th floor
Artillery House
Artillery Row
London SW1P 1RT
Telephone: 071-401 2280

**The Vocational Guidance Association**
7 Harley House
Upper Harley Street
London NW1 4RP
Telephone: 071-935 2600

# General business courses

**Business and Technology Education Council**
Central House
Upper Woburn Place
London WC1H 0HH
Telephone: 071-387 4141

# Professional associations

**Chartered Association of Certified Accountants**
29 Lincoln's Inn Fields
London WC2A 3EE
Telephone: 071-242 6855

## Chartered Building Societies Institute
19 Baldock Street
Ware SG12 9DH
Telephone: 0920 465051

## Chartered Institute of Bankers
10 Lombard Street
London EC3 9AS
Telephone: 071-623 3531

## Chartered Institute of Management Accountants
93 Portland Place
London W1N 4AB
Telephone: 071-637 2311

## Chartered Institute of Marketing
Moor Hall
Cookham
Maidenhead
Berkshire SL6 9QH
Telephone: 06285 24922

## Chartered Institute of Public Finance and Accountancy
3 Robert Street
London WC2N 6BH
Telephone: 071-930 3456

## Chartered Insurance Institute
20 Aldermanbury
London EC2V 7HY
Telephone: 071-606 3835

## Hotel Catering and Institutional Management Association
191 Trinity Road
London SW17 7HN
Telephone: 081-672 4251

## Institute of Administrative Management
40 Chatsworth Parade
Petts Wood
Orpington
Kent BR5 1RW
Telephone: 0689 75555

**Institute of Chartered Secretaries and Administrators**
16 Park Crescent
London W1N 4AH
Telephone: 071-580 4741

**Institute of Health Services Management**
75 Portland Place
London W1N 4AN
Telephone: 071-580 5041

**Institute of Leisure and Amenity Management**
Lower Basildon
Reading
Berkshire RG8 9NE
Telephone: 0491 873558

**Institute of Linguists**
24A Highbury Grove
London N5 2EA
Telephone: 071-359 7445

**Institute of Personnel Management**
IPM House
Camp Road
Wimbledon
London SW19 4UX
Telephone: 081-946 9100

**Institute of Purchasing and Supply**
Easton House
Easton on the Hill
Stamford
Lincolnshire PE9 3NZ
Telephone: 0780 56777

**Institute of Training and Development**
Marlow House
Institute Road
Marlow
Buckinghamshire
Telephone: 0628 890123

# Index